THE GOSPEL ACCORDING TO SPIRITISM
For Young Adults and Beginners

Laura Bergallo

COLLABORATION:
Gilberto Perez Cardoso

Translated to English by: **Spiritist Alliance for Books, Inc.**

Original Title: O Evangelho Segundo o Espiritismo para Jovens (2009) –Editora Lachatre – Sao Paulo - Brazil

Main entry under title:
THE GOSPEL ACCORDING TO SPIRITISM For Young Adults and Beginners

1. Religious Philosophy 2. Spiritist Doctrine 3. Christianity

Translated by SAB's Team: Jussara Korngold, Celina Pinto, Lorena Suppa Pereira Leandro and Armin Hanemann Junior
Cover Drawing and Design: Glaucia de Barros

Edited and revised by the Editorial and Publishing Department of the Spiritist Group of New York (SGNY) and the Spiritist Alliance for Books (SAB) 2010.

The Spiritist Alliance for Books (SAB) is a non-profit organization, which has the sole aim to promote and disseminate the Spiritist Doctrine in English, as codified by Allan Kardec.
SAB was officially established on April 12th, 2001. However, some of its participants have been earnestly fostering the dissemination of Spiritism in the United States and in the United Kingdom for over sixteen years.
The Spiritist Alliance for Books (SAB) is an organization that aims to unite people from all over the world who are willing to volunteer in the effort of translating spiritist books (which were originally written in other languages) into English.

Neither do people light a lamp and put it under a bowl. Instead they put it on its stand, and it gives light to everyone in the house.
(Mathew, chapter 5: 15)

To all those who long for the light of understanding

THE GOSPEL ACCORDING TO SPIRITISM
For Young Adults and Beginners

Reasons for resignation
Suicide and madness
In this chapter, the spirits teach

The gentle yoke
The promised consoler
In this chapter, the spirits teach

What does "poor in spirit" mean?
He who exalts himself shall be humbled
Mysteries are hidden from the learned and prudent
In this chapter the spirits teach

Simplicity and pureness of heart
Sinning by means of thought: Adultery
True pureness – Unwashed hands
Offences – If your hand be the cause of an offence, cut it off.
In this chapter the spirits teach
In this chapter Kardec teaches

Insults and violence
In this chapter the spirits teach

Forgive others so that God may forgive you
Reconciliation with your adversaries
The sacrifice most agreeable to God
The speck and the beam in the eye
Do not judge others if you do not wish to be judged in return – he that
is without a sin let him be the first to cast a stone
In this chapter, the spirits teach

Give to Caesar that which belongs to Caesar
In this chapter, the spirits teach

The courage of faith
Carry your cross – He who will save his life shall lose it

Help yourself and heaven will help you
Look at the birds of the air
Provide not gold in your purse

The gift of healing
Paid prayers
The merchants expelled from the temple

The characteristics of prayer
The effectiveness of prayer
The action of prayer – Transmission of thought
Intelligible prayers
Prayers for the dead and for suffering spirits
In this chapter, spirits teach

PREFACE TO THE ENGLISH EDITION

Despite the many manners of interpreting Jesus' teachings, which vary according to the different religions based on him, the moral taught by Jesus should not be a reason for disputes. Starting with this premise, Allan Kardec, the originator of Spiritism, with the help of the spirits that accompanied him in his work, analyzed the most important and some of the most controversial teachings of Jesus. In this manner "The Gospel According to Spiritism," one of the most important works of the Spiritist philosophy, was born.

Over the years, the knowledge imparted in this book enriched my life in ways I cannot describe. As a natural consequence and, most importantly as a mother, I envisioned the impact a version of this book, primed specially for young people, would have. As a practicing Spiritist, I would like nothing better than to provide children and teens with an opportunity to benefit from its wealth of knowledge and inspiration as I did.

Though initially written for the adult audience, after a brilliant adaptation by Laura Bergallo, "The Gospel According to Spiritism for Young Adults and Beginners," was finally released in 2009.

Understandably, the effort to convert the language to simpler terms could not be an easy task. We are all indebted to Ms. Bergallo for accepting the challenge, and now, for allowing us the opportunity to publish it in English.

It is my sincere hope that this version brings to parents in all English-speaking countries the same joy and fulfillment that I'm sure it will bring to my fourteen year-old son, Gabriel.

New York, 2010
Jussara Korngold,

Spiritist Group of New York, Inc. - Founder and President
Spiritist Alliance for Books, Inc. - Founder and President

ALLAN KARDEC
AND THE GOSPEL ACCORDING TO SPIRITISM

The professor, pedagogue and French writer Hippolyte Leon Denizard Rivail (1804), whose pseudonym was Allan Kardec was the codifier of Spiritism. He was responsible for translating a doctrine transmitted by discarnate spirits into words that includes three basic aspects of human knowledge, philosophy, science and religion.

"The Spirits' Book" was the beginning of everything. It specially brought the philosophical side of Spiritism. "The Medium's Book" was the work in which Kardec transcribed spiritual information that clarifies phenomena such as mediumship and communication between 'live' people and spirits of 'dead' people, among others, which are linked to the scientific aspect of Spiritism. At last "The Gospel According to Spiritism" is his utterly religious and moral work, whose story is summarized below.

While preparing the draft of what would be the "The Gospel According to Spiritism", in August 1863, Kardec queried a Spirit (without the medium's knowledge) about the work he had been organizing secretly. The secrecy was also extended to the title, which the editor just came to know at the time of printing. The spirit replied that the work would be of significant importance, not only in the religious world but also for practical real life.

This spirit said long ago that Good Spirits have been planning the releasing of this book, which would have the aim of rescuing people from obscurity and free them from moral ignorance. The spirit also revealed that both of them (the entity that was communicating and Kardec himself) have been working on the Spirituality long enough in order to issue this work into the physical plan. Kardec was told that the book's releasing would arouse great opposition from established religions; however he could count on Spirits' support for such a hard mission.

Thus, the first edition of "The Gospel According to Spiritism" appeared in April 1864 but under another name,

"L'Imitation de l'Evangile Selon L'Espiritism" or "The Imitation of the Gospel According to Spiritism." At the suggestion of the editor, Mr. Didier and other fellows of the Doctrine, Kardec has yet changed the title in the second edition in 1865 for "The Gospel According to Spiritism".

The issue that prompts us to compose "The Gospel According to Spiritism for Young Adults and Beginners" is the third French edition of 1866.

First in the introduction of "The Gospel According to Spiritism", we can find Kardec's explanations about the purpose of the work and clarification on the authority of Spiritism, apart from the meaning of many words frequently used in the Gospel texts, in order to simplify the reader's understanding for the true meaning of certain maxims of Christ, which at first glance may seem strange. Also in the introduction, Kardec makes references to Socrates and Plato as forerunners of Christian Doctrine and Spiritism.

"The Gospel According to Spiritism" is composed of 28 chapters, 27 of which are devoted to the explanation of the maxims of Jesus, his concern with the Spiritism and its application to various situations of life. The last chapter consists of a collection of spiritist prayers.

The work is remarkable and has been widespread since its publishing nearly 150 years ago, and has already been translated into several languages. It is an advanced moral code, and has the advantage of clarifying many puzzling passages of the Gospel, when examined under the light of the spiritist interpretation.

"The Gospel According to Spiritism" is, along with "The Spirits' Book", a milestone in the consolidation of Spiritism in the world. We hope that our "The Gospel According to Spiritism for Young Adults and Beginners" may provide a contribution to its propagation, especially among younger readers.

Rio de Janeiro, May 2008
Laura Bergallo and Gilberto Perez Cardoso

HOW THIS BOOK CAME TO LIFE

How was this book born? The idea of the current book was born years ago when we were studying "The Spirits' Book" at our family meeting with the children, then pre-teens. After studying good spiritist works for children, we decided to head for "The Spirits' Book". Of course, the questions and answers had to be summarized, explained and adapted to the young's understanding, because the language used by Kardec and the Spirits who reported was of difficult comprehension for this age group. Our conclusion was that a written adaptation of "The Spirits' Book " could be very useful for the dissemination of Spiritism among the young, not only in spiritist youth, but also in the spiritist education activities and home studies.

Then "The Little Spirits' Book for Young Adults and Beginners" was published. It was a countrywide editorial success, an adaptation made by Laura, a specialized writer in works for children and young people of "The Spirits' Book."

At that time, soon after "The Little Spirits' Book for Young Adults and Beginners" *was* released and due to its excellent acceptance by the general public (not just the young), we began to receive requests from readers who asked that "The Gospel According to Spiritism" could also earn an adaptation especially intended for the young reader, providing an easy access and understanding of young people to this important work of Kardec. It was not an easy task, but we accepted the challenge, and now we bring into public "The Gospel According to Spiritism for Young Adults and Beginners".

As we have also warned in the adaptation of "The Spirits' Book", this current adjustment does not aim to replace the wonderful "The Gospel According to Spiritism", it just addresses to briefly present it in an updated and straight language to the young reader who isn't willing, for any other reason, to venture on more than 300 pages of the original version.

The book was written according to an applied method in order to make its reading as pleasant as possible and also to have its contents as didactic as possible.

Thus, we conventionally kept original all the chapter headings and all quotations of the Gospel used by Kardec, but fixing on maximum updating of the ancient language held in the scriptures in an effort to bring the Gospel text to the universe of the 21st Century young. Having this goal, for example, we made some changes we regarded necessary.[1]

Similarly, we chose to summarize Kardec's comments and synthesize the spirit's instructions in each chapter, without appointing them by the name, once those directions are consistent and what matters is (according to what the spirits had taught us) its content. Both Kardec's comments and the spirit's instructions also had their language adapted and updated to make the comprehension easier for the young and new public.

Kardec in the Spiritist Magazine published most of the Spiritist messages that gave rise to "The Gospel According to Spiritism". Among the Spirits whose posts are quoted in "The Gospel According to Spiritism" are those who identify more vaguely, signing as a "guardian spirit" or "a familiar spirit". However, others are well known, and belong to the field of arts, literature, philosophy, theology or even science, like Fenelon, Erastus, Lacordaire, John the Baptist, Lazarus, Hahnemann, Apostle Paul, Pascal, Lamennais. Curious are the messages given by the Spirit Emmanuel (who would probably be our Emmanuel - Chico Xavier's mentor) and the messages given by those considered "saints" in Catholic theology, such as St. Louis and St. Augustine (who, in addition, enters into "The Gospel According to Spiritism" with many messages). St. Augustine himself explains that, as discarnate, his vision has expanded. That made him understand in a broader range what he had preached as a Catholic bishop when incarnate in Hippo; when discarnate, he labored very hard for the

---

[1] TN: The author made the changes in the Portuguese version. For the English Version we used the New International Version from BibleGateway.com.

work to come to light by Kardec's writing. The messages signed by the "Spirit of Truth" are outstanding, and some claim to be from Christ himself.

Within the method adopted by us, we did not include the 28th and last chapter, because they are specific chapters on prayers that may be consulted by the reader whenever he or she wants to find inspiration for a specific model of prayer. It is good to remember Kardec's advice not to take any standardization in Spiritism. Therefore, the prayers inserted by the codifier intends to serve only as a model in which people can be inspired when they want to pray.

Here it is, then, dear reader, the result of our efforts on trying to bring you this wonderful content that can be found in the pages of "The Gospel According to Spiritism". We are hoping that "The Gospel According to Spiritism for Young Adults and Beginners" arises in a pleasant and edifying reading for you and may encourage you to dive into the fountain of such necessary knowledge for the current phase of our world of tests and atonements.

Rio de Janeiro, May 2008

Gilberto Perez Cardoso

I HAVE NOT COME TO DESTROY THE LAW

"Do not think that I have come to abolish the Law or the Prophets; I have not come to abolish them but to fulfill them. I tell you the truth, until heaven and earth disappear, not the smallest letter, not the least stroke of a pen, will by any means disappear from the Law until everything is accomplished. (Matthew, chapter 5: 17-18)

The three revelations – Moses, Christ, Spiritism
The first revelation

The law Moses revealed to the world came in two parts: the Law of God announced on Mount Sinai and the Civil Law, which mandated certain behaviors and forbade others. Moses revealed the Civil Law himself and the combination of the two would come to constitute what we call the *First Revelation*.

The Law of God, as revealed to Moses and, through him, to all humanity consisted of Ten Commandments. These do not vary with respect to time or space. No matter what the epoch or region or ethnic variety or culture, these stand immutable.

On the other hand, the Civil Law, according to which behaviors were either mandated or forbidden, do change - at least in terms of how they are interpreted and applied - from one world view to the next, from this land to that, from these people to those; for this law is temporal. It is human's law, not God's.

In the time of Moses, these Ten Commandments had to be rigorously enforced and interpreted to the very 'letter of the law' because the people of that time were still very primitive and unruly. In other words, Moses had to deliver these commandments to his people as sternly as possible precisely because his followers so sorely needed this kind of discipline in order to become a more civilized people.

Rigorous obedience to these laws, however, would be less and less important as human beings evolved.

The second revelation

Jesus himself brought us *The Second Revelation* thousands of years later simply by talking to people and acting as an example of what he taught. Through Jesus' words and actions this second revelation made changes in parts of the first; explained what had been confusing in it; and let us know that we could communicate with God straightforwardly - no rituals had ever or would ever be required.

Finally, as part of this revelation, Jesus summarized all the commandments Moses had given us in a single law expressed in just one sentence: "Love God above all things and your neighbor as yourself." By saying these words, he taught us that we should strive to understand and follow God's most important law, for within it was the essence of all that had come before.

He also explained that our real lives were not the ones lived on earth, but rather the ones we live in the kingdom of God. And, finally, he said that He had come to the world precisely to show us how to reach this life and how to make amends with God in order to live in peace with him in his kingdom.

There was a great deal, however, that Jesus could not reveal to us at that time, so he made it very clear that, only later, when humanity was ready, would certain subjects be explained. He declared, in fact, that only when humanity had developed enough to understand much more in scientific terms, would it be ready to understand the Third Revelation, which would come to be known as Spiritism.

The third revelation

Spiritism, or the *Third Revelation*, is a new, more complete form of science that explains the existence of the spirits, the spiritual world and its relationship to the material world. Spiritism shows us that this spiritual world is the source of much that has gone understood and that it, too, is part of nature. It follows, therefore, that there is no such thing as the 'supernatural'; everything can be understood.

Although, Moses personified the First Revelation as found in the Old Testament and Jesus personified the Second as described in the New Testament, Spiritism, which came to humanity as the Third Revelation, would not be represented by a single human being because Spiritism was revealed through many spirits and channeled through many different mediums.

Spiritism teaches nothing contrary to Jesus' teachings. Rather, it explains His teachings by making explicit what was taught in allegorical (or symbolic) terms. These straightforward teachings demystify and clarify important concepts making them much easier to grasp.

Jesus sent us Spiritism (the work of all those spirits and mediums) to help us prepare ourselves to be part of the World of Regeneration, which the earth is already in the process of becoming. By the time the transformation has been completed, earth's inhabitants will have reached a point in their evolution, which will have brought them much closer to a true understanding of their condition as immortal spirits.

The alliance between science and religion

Science and religion are the two engines of human intelligence, one revealing the laws of the material world, the other the laws of the moral world. Since they both came from God they cannot be incompatible. The apparent incongruity between them only exists in the minds of those who, on one side or the other - since they preside exclusively over the religious or the scientific realm, never both - want to believe that the truth their discipline encompasses, whatever it may be, is the whole truth, and that anything outside of that must be fantasy.

The fact is that science and religion are actually complementary and the time has come for science to start accepting the reality of the spiritual world and for religion to recognize the primacy of science in the understanding of the natural world and the laws that govern it.

The fundamental disconnection between science and religion is due to the fact that science has not yet been able to acknowledge or even understand the fact that the laws that govern the spiritual world and the ways in which it interacts with the material world are as real and objective as the laws of physics or biology.

When this great revolution that has counted on the dedicated collaboration of several highly evolved spirits over the course of eighteen centuries is finally complete, it will have ushered in a New Age for all humankind. Every aspect of human existence, including the very fabric of intrapersonal relationships will have been transformed, for the Law of Progress - as ceaseless and unchanging as every other divine law - governs all of our relationships.

In this chapter the spirits teach:

1. That Moses started a process that would be continued by Jesus and completed by Spiritism.

2. That the laws of Moses were only as rigorous as they were because the people of that time were still very primitive in terms of their moral development.

3. That those who embrace Spiritism should work tirelessly to teach people everywhere this translation of Christ's thoughts and teachings so that they can one day be grasped and practiced the world over.

CHAPTER 2

MY KINGDOM IS NOT OF THIS WORLD

Pilate then went back inside the palace, summoned Jesus and asked him, "Are you the king of the Jews?" Jesus said, "My kingdom is not of this world. If it were, my servants would fight to prevent my arrest by the Jews. But now my kingdom is from another place." "You are a king, then!" said Pilate. Jesus answered, "You are right in saying I am a king. In fact, for this reason I was born, and for this I came into the world, to testify to the truth. Everyone on the side of truth listens to me." (John, chapter 18: 33, 36 e 37)

The future life

What Jesus said about his kingdom not being of this world, the words used as the title of this chapter, refer to the future life. The future life should actually be our highest priority, the highest objective of humanity.

Before Jesus came, the Jews' ideas about life after death were not very clear. They believed in angels, whom they considered to be very powerful, but they didn't know that all people can become angels one day. They also thought that the rewards reserved to those who followed God's laws would always be restricted to material goods, physical health, and military victories. In fact, whenever they lost battles or suffered other calamities, they thought God was punishing them for not following His laws.

The people whom Moses led at that time were ignorant of spiritual matters and still gauged the value of their lives on the basis of whether or not they had achieved material success. The fact that there would be an afterlife, during which bad deeds would be punished and good deeds rewarded, would not be revealed to them for a long time. The idea, in fact, that good deeds would be rewarded in non-material ways - unrelated to anything they had ever known on earth - would have been completely incomprehensible.

It was, in fact, precisely because of the still relatively limited spiritual perspective of the people around him, that Jesus, all those many years later, could not reveal everything that characterized that future life. Thus, he limited himself to presenting the future life in principle, as a law of nature, from which no one could escape. Consequently, the concept that the people of Jesus' time had of the future life was still quite vague.

When humanity finally matured enough, Spiritism was revealed to complete the teachings of Christ. It was with the coming of Spiritism that life after death was finally understood as a concrete reality. Channeled Spirits described the nature of their lives and the environments in which they were living in minute detail. They revealed that there were happy and unhappy places where people went according to the choices they had made on earth. This made the existence of Divine Justice much easier to understand.

The kingship of Jesus

At this point, it is essential that we be clear about the kingship attributed to Jesus Christ. It cannot be interpreted to be anything like the majesty conferred upon the kings who rule on earth. Christ's kingship refers to the high position He holds in spiritual terms, and His power to influence human progress.

It is the kind of royalty that can only be attained through personal merit and has much more meaning than kingship on earth, which does not always reflect the personal merit of the sovereign. It is in this sense that we should understand Jesus' answer to Pilate: "I am king, but my kingdom is not of this world."

A point of view

The reason our concept of the future life or hereafter is fundamental to our spiritual evolution, is that it so greatly influences the way we think about our earthly (material) existence. Those who firmly believe in spiritual life see their lives on earth as a passing phase and are therefore able to handle the problems and suffering of material life with patience, knowing not only that these hardships are transitory, but that they will be followed by a much happier life. These fortunate people are not afraid of death because they see it as a door to freedom.

On the other hand, anyone who doubts that other life cannot help but focus exclusively on their earthly life. Since they cannot accept the existence of anything beyond matter, the possibility of anything better is not something they can even imagine. Any loss, therefore, or mistake, or injustice has a much greater impact on them; so much so that they go to great lengths to torment themselves when anything goes wrong, particularly if it involves a blow to their vanity or pride. Furthermore, since they can only value what is material, any material loss seems terribly serious to them.

The importance given to earthly goods varies inversely to the strength of one's faith in the other life. In other words, anyone who really believes in life after death doesn't worry too much over their lives on earth and has an easier time dealing with problems or even failure, because they know what awaits them once they've discarnated (left their organic bodies).

But God does not condemn the pleasures and joys of the flesh; what He does condemn is the abuse of such pleasures when it causes one to forget the concerns of one's soul. The individual who identifies with the other (the spiritual) life is like the wealthy person who doesn't fret over small monetary losses, since one has so much more; while the individual who believes only in earthly life is like the poverty-stricken who despair over each small loss.

Spiritism gives us larger things to think about and widens our horizons. It shows that our lives on earth are no more than a moment lost in eternity. Furthermore, it explains the solidarity, which connects those who exist on a single plane of existence as well as those inhabiting any number of different worlds.

In this chapter the spirits teach:

1. That greed for material goods is unworthy of us, since all earthly illusions disappear in spiritual life.

2. That the only things we need to work in order to ensure our place in the next life are selflessness, humility, charity, and benevolence toward all beings.

CHAPTER 3

IN MY FATHER'S HOUSE ARE MANY MANSIONS

"Do not let your hearts be troubled. Trust in God; trust also in me. In my Father's house are many rooms; if it were not so, I would have told you. I am going there to prepare a place for you. And if I go and prepare a place for you, I will come back and take you to be with me that you also may be where I am. (John, chapter 14: 1-3)

The different states of the soul in the errant[1] state

The house Jesus called "My Father's House" was actually the universe. The different mansions are the various worlds within it on which spirits can incarnate. These worlds are more or less advanced depending on the level of evolution already attained by their inhabitants. In other words, these worlds are more advanced if those who inhabit them are also more advanced and less advanced if their inhabitants are more primitive spirits.

But Jesus' words may also be understood as referring to the happy or unhappy situation of the spirit in the errant state, where advanced, average or delayed (somewhat primitive) spirits may gather. In these spheres each spirit becomes aware of its position in spiritual life and many times creates a more permanent environment for itself, beyond physical reality, which corresponds in its nature to the level of spiritual advancement the spirit has attained.

In a way, these non-physical environments, which are not limited by frontiers, (whether happy or unhappy) is actually within the spirit itself.

---

[1] The situation of errant spirits, that is, not incarnate, during the intervals between their corporeal existences. – TR.

The different categories of inhabited worlds

Spirits tell us that there are worlds similar to our planet earth and others that are more or less advanced than our planet both physically and morally. The inhabitants of inferior worlds give infinitely more importance to their material reality; they are still quite primitive, morally and spiritually. On more advanced worlds, material objects are much less important; inhabitants there tend to focus on spiritual life. On intermediate worlds, there is a mixture of good and evil, with the predominance of one or the other, depending on the level of evolution, which characterizes the majority of the world's inhabitants.

Based on the above classifications, worlds can be termed primitive (those on which human beings live their very first lives), worlds of tests and atonements (where evil is still dominant), regenerative worlds (where painful periods are balanced by periods of happiness or rest from the toil of daily life), happy worlds (where the good outweighs evil) and, finally, heavenly or divine worlds (where good reigns completely and only spirits who have redeemed and regenerated themselves live).

Earth's destiny

Our planet, in terms of the classification system explained in *The Spirits' Book*, is still a world of Tests and Atonements. This classification means that here on earth conflicts, tragedies and miseries are more the rule than the exception.

But spirits don't reincarnate on the same planet forever. As they progress, they come to reincarnate on progressively more evolved planets until they finally become pure spirits. As they progress and start to live in more advanced worlds they get really happy because living on more primitive worlds where there is so more much unhappiness is like a kind of punishment to them.

And the earth itself, just like every other world, is evolving. Some time from now it will cease to be a planet dedicated to Tests and Atonements and finally become a world where the theme is regeneration.

The cause of earthly misery

Many people are shocked by the cruelty, diseases and poverty on earth and end up thinking that humankind is still very primitive. But we should remember that not all of humanity is on this one planet. The part of humanity that is on our planet is only a small fraction of the human species, for humanity is the species that includes all rational beings living on every planet and every world that exists in the entire universe. Taking this into consideration it's easier to see that the population of our planet is but a small part of humanity as a whole.

Analogously, we could say that if we went to a hospital we would only see the sick; if we went to a prison we would only see criminals. If we imagine that the earth is a kind of hospital or prison and remember that not all the inhabitants of a city are in a hospital or a prison, we'll understand that not all of humanity is here on earth, because only those who need to be on earth - temporarily - are living here now. And, just as the sick leave the hospital when they are well enough to do so, those who live on earth leave this planet for much happier worlds as soon as they are well enough, having recovered from spiritual or moral maladies.

In this chapter the spirits teach:
(About the superior and inferior worlds)

1. That the classification of different worlds as superior or inferior depends on how they compare with other worlds.

2. That the more advanced a world is, the greater the longevity enjoyed by its people; that the death of these morally

superior beings, who inhabit more advanced planets is gentle since their bodies do not have to decompose, but rather, simply transform themselves.

3. That in more advanced worlds, spirits live in less material bodies (not in the least like our heavy, primitive bodies) and are able to leave their bodies and return to them while fully conscious according to the dictates of their own needs or desires.

4. That in these worlds, relationships between various groups are peaceful since there are no tyrants, slaves, or undeserved privileges.

5. That in these worlds, there is only intellectual or moral superiority (in other words, no one is better than anyone else on the basis of wealth, physical strength, beauty or even power, but rather, for being wiser or kinder.

6. That on these worlds, authority is respected by all because the kind of authority there is on these planets is based exclusively on merit as determined through the use of just criteria by careful judges.

7. That the inhabitants of these more advanced worlds don't fight to conquer or defeat others; but rather struggle within themselves in order to become better people than they already are. That their battles, therefore, are waged against the temptation to become self-satisfied, which would get in the way of their struggle to evolve and their goal is to conquer a place among pure spirits (and to this goal they dedicate themselves completely).

8. That there is no great suffering in this struggle to reach the state of pure spirits, for it is comprised of intensive study, work and dedication.

9. That in such advanced worlds kindness and other similar feelings are recognized, cultivated, even stimulated. That, in fact, on these planets, there is no hate, competition, envy or conflict between inhabitants, for they are all connected exclusively by love and fraternity, such that those who are stronger, or more advanced help the weaker ones among them.

10. That in these worlds, each individual possesses comforts and other goods in accordance to the amount of intelligence, dedication, and hard work invested in acquiring them. On the other hand, unlike the situation on earth, on more advanced worlds, those who are not able to earn these comforts are not deprived of anything essential to their survival because on these planets there are no longer any spirits who need to redeem themselves by suffering (evil no longer exists).

11. That in these worlds, there are none of the contrasts we so often see here on earth where we still need the evils of darkness and disease in order to value health and light.

12. That these happy worlds are not, however, privileged planets, since God does not prefer one set of beings over others; that all those who wish to live on happier planets have the opportunity, all they need to do is want to progress and work hard toward that goal; that those who work hardest toward this goal achieve it first, and that those who give up on their struggle to evolve lag behind.

(About worlds of tests and atonements)

1. That the earth is not a primitive world, but is still in the category of worlds dedicated to tests and atonements.

2. That the human beings who are living on planet earth have already progressed to some degree but still have terrible flaws and make many mistakes. It is, in fact, for this very reason that they live on a planet where they will inevitably suffer and, thereby, be able to redeem themselves through the process of atonement before evolving to the point where, through their own efforts, they are able to reach a more advanced world.

3. That not all spirits who incarnate on earth are here for atonement purposes; that less advanced (primitive) peoples, for example, are here for educational purposes; that those who are still not as civilized as inhabitants of

industrialized nations like indigenous peoples have already made some progress.

4. That spirits, who are on earth for atonement have already lived on other planets from which they were exiled for having insisted on the practice of evil.

5. That the earth is suitable both for atonement - suffering the consequences of past mistakes - and exile for spirits who rebelled against the laws of God when they were living on more advanced planets.

6. That this exile helps the inhabitants of more primitive worlds to progress because the spirits who come from more advanced planets bring the less evolved spirits a great deal of knowledge (to which their more evolved intelligence has already contributed).

7. That spirits on earth must deal with human cruelty and the hardships of nature every day, but that this process helps them develop their intelligence as well as their hearts; in this way God uses suffering as an instrument for the development of the human spirit.

(About regenerative worlds)

1. That there are many worlds like ours in the universe, worlds that exist to house those who are still working on tests and atonements, and that many planetary systems include more advanced worlds as well as less advanced and intermediary ones. And also that these last, the intermediary or transitional worlds, are also called regenerative worlds.

2. That there are worlds where newly created spirits are placed even before they have learned about good and evil, so they can begin to make their way to God by using their free will (which is to say, their capacity to choose between good and evil).

3. That many spirits choose the lesser path and God allows them to follow their inclinations on less advanced worlds where incarnation by incarnation they can regenerate

themselves and then choose a better path so that they can one day get closer to God.

4. That the worlds of regeneration are transitional worlds where spirits prepare themselves to move from worlds of tests and atonements to happier worlds and that on these worlds the soul finds tranquility and enough rest to progress farther.

5. That on these worlds humanity is still limited by matter, but freer from lower passions like pride, envy and hate; that all inhabitants know God and there is equality in human relationships though there isn't yet perfect happiness (the spirit still has to contend with some trials but without the anguish of atonement).

6. That on these worlds the individual still makes mistakes and also, in a certain way, can be influenced by evil, so it has to advance with determination and make great effort to keep getting better because there is still the possibility of relapse and exile back to worlds of tests and atonements.

7. That for those who now live on earth, advancement to a regenerative world is a wonderful and joyous achievement in its own right.

(About the progression of worlds)

1. That worlds transform themselves continuously in order to adapt to the level of evolution attained by the majority of its inhabitants; the more advanced the world's inhabitants, the more pleasant it is to live on it.

2. That often, according to the law of progress that constantly expresses itself everywhere in nature, times of destruction are no more than periods of transformation.

3. That our world was once both materially and morally inferior to its current state and that it is about to rise through the progressive classification of worlds, for it is going through one of its periods of transformation.

4. That the earth will, in a short time, go from its period as a world of tests and atonements to a new period, a period of

regeneration, during which its human inhabitants will be happier as a result of this greater expression of the law of God.

CHAPTER 4

NO ONE CAN SEE THE KINGDOM OF GOD UNLESS HE IS BORN AGAIN

When Jesus came to the region of Caesarea Philippi, he asked his disciples, "Who do people say the Son of Man is?" They replied, "Some say John the Baptist; others say Elijah; and still others, Jeremiah or one of the prophets." "But what about you?" he asked. "Who do you say I am?" Simon Peter answered, "You are the Christ, the Son of the living God." Jesus replied, "Blessed are you, Simon son of Jonah, for this was not revealed to you by man, but by my Father in heaven. (Matthew, chapter 16: 13-17; Mark, chapter 8: 27-30)

King Herod heard about this, for Jesus' name had become well known. Some were saying, "John the Baptist has been raised from the dead, and that is why miraculous powers are at work in him." Others said, "He is Elijah." And still others claimed, "He is a prophet, like one of the prophets of long ago." But when Herod heard this, he said, "John, the man I beheaded, has been raised from the dead!" (Mark, chapter 6: 14-16; Luke, chapter 9: 7-9)

(After the transfiguration) The disciples asked him, "Why then do the teachers of the law say that Elijah must come first?" Jesus replied, "To be sure, Elijah comes and will restore all things. But I tell you, Elijah has already come, and they did not recognize him, but have done to him everything they wished. In the same way the Son of Man is going to suffer at their hands." Then the disciples understood that he was talking to them about John the Baptist. (Matthew, chapter 17: 10-13; Mark, chapter 9: 11-13)

Resurrection and reincarnation

In the time of Jesus, most of the Jews believed in reincarnation but there was no more than a rudimentary and incomplete idea of what the soul was and its connection to the physical body. They thought the dead could resuscitate but they didn't know how. They called the phenomenon 'resurrection', which, with greater accuracy, Spiritism calls reincarnation.

To explain this better, let us say that their concept of resurrection held that a dead body could come back to life - a phenomenon which science has held to be impossible, at least as far as is known to this day. Reincarnation, on the other hand refers to the return of a spirit to corporeal life in a newly formed body, completely distinct from its previous physical self.

> *Now there was a man of the Pharisees named Nicodemus, a member of the Jewish ruling council. He came to Jesus at night and said, "Rabbi, we know you are a teacher who has come from God. For no one could perform the miraculous signs you are doing if God were not with him." In reply Jesus declared, "I tell you the truth, no one can see the kingdom of God unless he is born again." "How can a man be born when he is old?" Nicodemus asked. "Surely he cannot enter a second time into his mother's womb to be born!" Jesus answered, "I tell you the truth, no one can enter the kingdom of God unless he is born of water and the Spirit. Flesh gives birth to flesh, but the Spirit gives birth to spirit. You should not be surprised at my saying, 'You must be born again.' The wind blows wherever it pleases. You hear its sound, but you cannot tell where it comes from or where it is going. So it is with everyone born of the Spirit." "How can this be?" Nicodemus asked. "You are Israel's teacher," said Jesus, "and do you not understand these things? I tell you the truth, we speak of what we know, and we testify to what we have seen, but still you people do not accept our testimony. I have spoken to you of earthly things and you do not believe; how then will you believe if I speak of heavenly things? (John, chapter 3: 1-12)*

The idea that John the Baptist was Elijah and that prophets could live again occurred in many passages of the Gospel and if it were a mistaken belief, Jesus would have said so. The exact opposite occurred: Jesus confirmed this credo, going so far as to say that being born again was a necessary step for the evolution of humankind. In His own words, "No one can see the Kingdom of God unless he is born again."

When Jesus said, "whatever is born from the flesh is flesh and what is born from spirit is spirit," he meant that only the body can be born from the body and that the spirit is independent of the body, which is to say that the spirit cannot become body. Another thing Jesus said about the spirit was, "you know not from whence it comes, nor where it goes," which meant that no one knew anything about what it was or would become. It also meant that the spirit exists since before the birth of the body, for if the spirit had been created at the same time as the body, we would know its origin.

> From the days of John the Baptist until now, the kingdom of heaven has been forcefully advancing, and forceful men lay hold of it. For all the Prophets and the Law prophesied until John. And if you are willing to accept it, he is the Elijah who was to come. He who has ears, let him hear. (Matthew, chapter 11: 12-15)

This passage leaves no room for doubt about the existence of reincarnation: "he is, in fact, the very Elijah who is to come". In other words, according to Jesus, John the Baptist was Elijah reincarnated. The violence described in the text speaks truths contained in the Law of Moses, which, as we already know, was very rigorous, even ordering death to the "infidels," the new law, the one taught by Jesus, preached charity, even meekness. But when he said that those who had ears to hear should listen, he meant that not everyone was ready to understand his messages.

> But your dead will live; their bodies will rise. You who dwell in the dust, wake up and shout for joy. Your dew is like the dew of the morning; the earth will give birth to her dead. (Isaiah, chapter 26: 19)

In this passage Isaiah was again referring to reincarnation. If he had only meant to speak of spiritual life, he would have said that the dead "still live" and not "that they will live again." By saying, "they will live again," he meant that they would reincarnate.

> But man dies and is laid low; he breathes his last and is no more. As water disappears from the sea or a riverbed becomes parched and dry, so man lies down and does not rise; till the heavens are no more, men will not awake or be roused from their sleep. "If only you would hide me in the grave and conceal me till your anger has passed! If only you would set me a time and then remember me! If a man dies, will he live again? All the days of my hard service I will wait for my renewal to come. (Job, chapter 14: 10-14)

In this passage Job was clearly talking about the principle of reincarnation. In the struggle known as daily life, he resigned himself to his troubles and waited for change to occur. In other word, after his death, during the time he had between one corporeal existence and the next, he would wait for the moment of return to a physical body for his reincarnation.

Although they called it *resurrection*, the principle of *reincarnation* was one of the Jews' most fundamental beliefs. Only reincarnation could tell humans where they had come from, where they were going, why they were on earth, and also justify the conflicts and all the (apparent) injustices, which human life presented.

The principles of reincarnation and the plurality of existences (or many incarnations) of the spirit were very important to a real understanding of the Gospel.

Family ties strengthened by reincarnation but severed by a single existence

Reincarnation strengthens family ties. In space (spiritual life) spirits form groups or families connected by affection or affinity, as well as by similar tastes and preferences.

Incarnation only separates these spirits for a moment in eternity, for when they return to space they reunite like old friends on the return from a voyage.

Many times some will follow others of their group through successive incarnations. The fact that some are incarnated at a particular time while others are still in space does not mean that they are really separated, for they are connected by thought. Those who are free, look after those on earth; the more advanced among them guide those who've been delayed in their progress, cheering them on.

This latter, long lasting tie of affection, which connects so many relatives, is so strong it will often not only outlast physical life, but also the life beyond it, for it can connect spirits through the course of many lifetimes. In fact, when such really deep ties exist between family members on earth it is often the case that that they were established several lifetimes before their current incarnations.

On the other hand, it is not uncommon for spirits who are strangers or even enemies to incarnate together. God allows this for two reasons: one is that this often-difficult coexistence can be both a trial for some and a chance to progress for others. The bad habits of the less evolved begin to lose their hold from their constant interactions with the more advanced spirits among them who are dedicated to benevolence and spiritual growth. Secondly, with this gradual lessening of hostilities between them their enmity can finally become quite mild. It is thus that the fusion amongst different categories of spirits is established, as occurs on the earth amongst ethnicities and cultures.

Clearly then, there would be no reason to worship one's ancestors. As for the future, if we believe that a person's destiny is determined after just one life many spirits would be irremediably and eternally separated and unable to find one another after death and fathers, mothers, sons, husbands, wives, brothers, sisters and friends would never be able to see one another again. In other words, if we lived only one life familial ties would be definitively broken at death, whereas, given the phenomenon of reincarnation and the ensuing progress of all spirits, all those who truly love one another meet again both on earth and in space making their way toward God together. Only reincarnation allows for eternal solidarity between human beings.

In this chapter the spirits teach:

1. That the physical body becomes progressively less material as the spirit is purified; that the more the spirit evolves, the greater the dematerialization of the body, which becomes almost like a fluid sort of vapor at which point it may even be mistaken for the perispirit (the spirits' almost weightless envelope, which follows it everywhere) or spiritual body.

2. That the perispirit itself goes through successive transformations, becoming more and more ethereal as it evolves until the spirit reaches the state of perfect spirits.

3. That during the time between incarnations, while the spirit is not in a physical body, the life it leads depends on its level of spiritual evolution, because that is what connects the spirit to more advanced or relatively primitive worlds.

4. That the passage spirits go through during their incarnate lives is necessary for the completion of the tasks given them by God, which also serve the purpose of further developing their intelligence.

5. That God established a basic level of moral/intellectual development with which He endowed every spirit as a point of departure, as well as the same tasks to perform and the same freedom of choice as to how to behave,

without ever giving any spirit any kind of preferential treatment.

6. That incarnation is only a passing phase spirits go through. That those who make good use of their free will evolve quickly, while those who misuse their freedom delay their progress. Furthermore, if these last persist in their wrongdoing, they may have to reincarnate many, many times... to spirits like these reincarnation eventually becomes a kind of punishment in and of itself.

In this chapter Kardec teaches:

1. That a spirit's development can be compared to the successive achievements of a student at school; the more basic classes prepare a dedicated student for more advanced ones and if one works hard one will reach one's goal much faster; while the student who wastes one's time delays one's progress and sometimes even has to start all over again as if one had been made to repeat the school year the student had just completed.

2. That while for more primitive spirits incarnation presents wonderful opportunities to develop intellect, for more advanced spirits it is a torment because they are forced to remain much longer in worlds which seem less developed than they are and provide much fewer opportunities for happiness.

3. That all incarnations serve a purpose. Even the short life of a child is useful as a test or atonement for both the child and its parents. It is an opportunity to make amends for damage they inflicted on one another in the past and to create a new spiritual foundation for the ties that hold their family together.

BLESSED ARE THE AFFLICTED

Blessed are those who mourn, for they will be comforted. Blessed are those who hunger and thirst for righteousness, for they will be filled. Blessed are those who are persecuted because of righteousness, for theirs is the kingdom of heaven. (Matthew, chapter 5: 4, 6 e 10)

"Blessed are you who are poor, for yours is the kingdom of God. Blessed are you who hunger now, for you will be satisfied. Blessed are you who weep now, for you will laugh. (Luke, chapter 6: 20-21)

"But woe to you who are rich, for you have already received your comfort. Woe to you who are well fed now, for you will go hungry. Woe to you who laugh now, for you will mourn and weep. (Luke, chapter 6: 24-25)

The justice of afflictions

The birth of some into poverty and others into wealth, as well as the suffering of kind souls juxtaposed to the victories of clearly cruel ones are the sorts of things which make much of what we see in life seem unjust, indeed, incomprehensible. But the only reason it seems so is that it cannot be understood until Jesus' words to the afflicted are proved to be true - and not in this life, but the next. Only then will it be possible to understand and accept the fact that suffering - and hence also the suffering of kind souls - is a blessing because it leads to bliss.

The contrasts we observe everyday might seem to be an example of God's injustice. But God is never unjust; on the contrary, He is infinitely just and perfect. He has power, kindness, and justice, as well as other qualities without which He would not be God. It would not be possible, therefore, for God to act unjustly or even preferentially. And so it follows that the unfortunate events that occur in people's lives have a reason for being - a reason, which must itself be just since God, is just. Now, God has revealed these causes to humanity through Spiritism, showing us all where our suffering began, its reason for being, and the purpose it serves.

Current causes of afflictions

Current suffering may either have originated in a past life or in the past of a current life. Many of the problems we have today are consequences of our personalities and related to our behavioral patterns.

We are, therefore, victims only of ourselves, of our pride, our carelessness, our ambition, our disorganization, our lack of foresight, and, finally, of our current choices and our current acts. We are our own victims because we are never satisfied with what we have, because vanity and self-interest characterize our relationships with others, because we fight for little or no reason, because we overindulge in food, drink, and other physical pleasures (which eventually lead to physical and mental illness if allowed to go on uncontrolled), and because we are careless and overindulgent in the way we bring up our children (who later react by being ungrateful or completely indifferent to us). We cause these and many other types of suffering in our lives simply by making the choices we make and acting the way we do.

If we were to think honestly about the origin of the problems that torment us, we would realize that, in most cases, they would not have occurred if we had only done or not done one thing or another. In other words, we would conclude that we ourselves were responsible for our problems. In many instances we have also caused the disharmony we notice in our relationships. But, since we are vain, instead of recognizing ourselves as responsible, we prefer to blame bad luck, God, or others for our problems. And so we forget that in order to solve these problems and avoid others, the solution is to work on improving ourselves, both morally and intellectually.

Suffering is a kind of warning to us that we have done something wrong. It gives us experience; helps us to distinguish the difference between good and evil more effectively and shows us how much we need to improve in order to avoid future suffering.

Sometimes when we realize this we think the warning and experience that suffering has brought us has reached us too late, after all the harm is done, but that is never the case. Just as each night brings a new day, people who have been in the dark always experience light again. There are always new lives to be lived and new opportunities to take advantage of the wisdom and experience gained through the hardships we are going through right now.

Prior causes of afflictions

But there are also problems that do not seem to have been caused by anything we have done or neglected to do in this life (things that seem to be no one's fault), like the death of those who are dear to us or on whom our whole family depend for sustenance. Other examples are accidents no one could have predicted, financial problems that come without warning, natural disasters (like earthquakes, hurricanes, and epidemics) and certain diseases or birth defects.

Some people are born with serious physical and/or mental disabilities. Others, even though the rest of their families enjoy good health, come to suffer from serious illnesses or even become disabled without having done anything in this life to deserve such misfortune.

There are also cases of children who die after living in pain since birth. In cases such as these, by believing the soul is created at the same time as the body we deny the existence of a just and merciful God. As a matter of fact, not a single philosophy or religion has been able to explain such misfortunes in this way. After all what could the children who died so soon after they were born have done to deserve such suffering? Why are they so harshly punished for mistakes they had no chance to make?

Since every effect must have a cause, such events must also have a cause; and if we believe God is just, the cause must also be just. Now, given that every cause precedes its effect (and, as previously discussed, the cause of a child's affliction cannot have occurred during that child's current life), the cause must lie in mistakes these children made in former lives.

Since God is justice, no one would suffer unless they had done something wrong or neglected to do something they should have done, if someone is suffering it must be because they have injured or persecuted someone somehow at some point in the past. It follows, therefore, that if someone was never cruel in this life they must have been so in some former existence.

Having this in mind, it becomes easy to understand why someone does not always make amends (not completely, at any rate) for what they do in this life before leaving it. What we can say with absolute certainty is that no one who has caused any harm to oneself or to others can escape from their consequences forever. And this consequence may come to pass in future lives, whether in whole or in part.

We can therefore, unequivocally affirm that an evil person's victories and prosperity are either merely apparent or very, very temporary. If one does not make amends today, one will atone for it tomorrow (in future lives). On the other hand, anyone suffering now is certain to be suffering the consequences of their own mistakes, even if they did not make them in this lifetime. All suffering, even if apparently undeserved, occurs for a reason.

Furthermore, there is a principle that is part and parcel of divine law, which guarantees that, due to God's infallible justice, every person will eventually suffer whatever one has made others suffer. If one's been harsh, one will be treated harshly; if one's been proud one will one day be born in humble circumstances; if one's been selfish or misused one's wealth, one may reincarnate in poverty and find little charity around oneself; if one's been uncaring as a son one will suffer the ingratitude of one's own children, and so forth.

Given that the earth is still a planet dedicated exclusively to tests and atonements, the distribution of fortune and misfortune as well as happiness and unhappiness among its inhabitants often seem arbitrary and inexplicable. But, as we can plainly see, everything has a logical explanation. So logically, each person should make a concerted effort to earn the right to be reborn in a more advanced world, where these great disparities no longer exist, because its inhabitants no longer need to atone or make amends

Tests and misfortunes may be imposed to hardened or ignorant spirits to help them growth. On the other hand, those who regret their mistakes and have gained enough insight to want to make amends for what they have done, will eventually even choose and request the kinds of trials and suffering they will have to endure in their next life.

Misfortunes can be useful either for atonement purposes - if past offenses merit suffering - or as tests of character that prepare a spirit for future lives. God, in his infinite mercy and justice, allows human beings to make amends for the hardships they have imposed on others. Not all suffering, though, is the result of past mistakes. It is often the case that spirits have requested certain kinds of problems in order to test themselves so they can make sure they have actually, fully acquired a virtue or mastered a set of skills. Solving problems is an excellent way to propel ourselves into spiritual progress. In fact, when a spirit reaches a certain level of evolution, it may choose to incarnate specifically in order to fulfill a mission or accomplish a difficult task. If it manages to completely fulfill its mission, it is rewarded.

This sort of path is often chosen by those who have good instincts, sensitivity, and benevolence. When we see someone who displays these qualities going through a difficult process without complaint - even exemplifying patience and resignation - it is almost always the case that the quiet martyrdom we have the privilege to witness is not atonement, but a test or mission chosen freely by the one we see enduring it with such awesome grace. Through this painful process the spirit grows immeasurably and clearly demonstrates the strength and fervor that drive it toward God, the good, and the further progress of its immortal spirit.

Spirits cannot consider themselves completely happy until they have finally become pure. If they are still imperfect they cannot reach the most blessed and accomplished worlds where most inhabitants are completely happy. So, as a spirit experiences hardship, one should be careful not to waste one's troubles by rebelling against them. It would be in the individual's best interest to make use of one's pain by accepting it and trying to learn from it. If one wastes the opportunity to learn from it, one may have to start all over again - not unlike a student who has to repeat a school year one's failed - and experience the troubles that have caused the person this suffering yet again.

Forgetfulness of the past

If we're to learn from experience, we might ask, why do we forget what happened to us and everything we did in our past lives? Our inability to remember past lives was established by God for our own good. Memory of past lives would bring great problems, because it would interfere with our free will (making it difficult for us to make our own decisions).

In nearly every case this kind of memory would also get in the way of our relationships with both family and friends since it is not the least bit unusual for a spirit to be reborn into the same circle of relatives and/or friends with whom one's already lived in the past so that the person can make amends to them, correcting the result of misfortunes one caused them. By relating to the same people within a family circle, the person can make up for the harm one has done them not only materially but spiritually as one repairs even the hearts and minds one broke in a former life. If the person had any inkling of what one had done before the hatred that had made one do it might have resurfaced in one's heart making it impossible for the person to reestablish the originally amicable relationships that once existed between oneself and these former companions.

So God in His wisdom determined that we would not remember our past lives, but that instead He would provide us with all we would need to live as peacefully as possible with our past enemies: the voice of conscience and the tendencies with which we each are born.

Truth be told, it's not particularly useful to know who we were before. All we need to know is that if we are undergoing any kind of suffering it is because we have been negligent or even cruel. What we need to do then is sincerely take stock of our current tendencies and work on whatever needs to be corrected. The voice of conscience speaking from within tells us which path to take and strengthens our ability to resist temptations that might otherwise lead us to make mistakes.

But this amnesia about our past lives only lasts until the end of our incarnate life. In other words, when our physical body dies, our spirit remembers its past lives again. It's akin to what happens to us during incarnate life when we wake up from a good night's rest; while sleeping we might have lived a different life, our dream life, but on waking we know reality once more. On the other hand, just as dreams may sometimes reflect reality, the spirit, even while incarnate, does not completely lose its memory of the past. Even while 'sleeping' in the incarnate state it is continuously aware of its acts. It also knows why it's suffering; and that no matter what one comes to suffer it is always deserved.

Reasons for resignation

Jesus' words show us that earthly suffering is always payment for debts incurred by mistakes made in the past and that, born with patience, this pain can save us centuries of

49

suffering in the future. This is how we should understand the words: *Blessed are those who mourn, for they will be comforted.*

Once the debt, which, through God's mercy, has usually been reduced to a fraction of what it originally was, the one who's just paid his debt is free. But should one refuses to bear one's troubles patiently and, eventually, even unfairly accuse God of being responsible for them one's situation will become even worst, because one will have to go through it all over again.

A human being can make one's earthly trials easier or harder to bear according to one's responses to them. In spiritual terms, life on earth is short. A firm conviction that a brighter future will come soon helps an incarnate spirit to overcome physical misfortune patiently and without complaint. If we face our troubles that way, the problems of our earthly lives come to be less important to us and we develop a talent for tranquility and resignation, which are always useful to both body and mind.

Suicide and madness

Tranquility and the ability to resign oneself to suffering - with the knowledge that 'this too shall pass' - are factors that help human beings avoid madness and suicide. A good many cases of madness come from emotional problems caused by misfortunes a spirit does not have the courage to face.

As for suicide, with the exception of those committed during episodes of drunkenness or psychosis - in which case it was committed beyond the bounds of rational thought - it tends to occur because of some kind of dissatisfaction.

People who are fully aware that their hardship is temporary are usually very patient, both withstanding and overcoming their problems much more easily, while everything is quite different for those who believe life ends with the death of the body. Since they don't expect there to be any kind of afterlife they often try to shorten the pain of their final days by committing suicide; but since life does, in fact, always go on, the attempt to end it always fails.

Spiritism is very helpful with regard to the problem of suicide because it lets us know exactly what happens to those who end their carnal lives that way. The spirits themselves tell their stories from the perspective of spiritual life. They tell us what they went through in the afterlife, describing it as abject misery, which proves that no one can subvert divine law unpunished.

Spiritists thus have several reasons to counterbalance the idea of suicide: the certainty of a better life to come, and the certainty that if they shorten their life they will in fact attain a worst result and will have more difficulties to meet their loved ones in the spiritual plane.

In this chapter, the spirits teach:

1. That we should be happy when we get an opportunity to struggle through periods of hardship and fight to overcome baser instincts, impatience, anger, and despair because, "blessed be those who suffer," means: blessed are those capable of proving their faith, fortitude, perseverance and acceptance of God's will on earth.

2. That the reason life on this planet can be so distressing is that most of its inhabitants are not spiritually evolved enough to be happy yet.

3. That we should console ourselves by thinking of the future that God is preparing for us, and that we need to look to our past for the reasons we suffer the hardships we are going through now.

4. That before reincarnating we choose many of the trials we are to go through ourselves, so we should suffer them patiently, without raging against God.

5. That the most healing balm we can use is faith, which always shines a light on the best path we can take to lessen our sorrows.

6.　　That we cannot expect to find real enduring happiness in this world, and that not even youth, wealth and power can ever be enough to bring us enduring happiness while on this planet.

7.　That the earth is not destined to be this penitentiary where we must 'do our time' forever.　That it will evolve (like humanity itself) and become a much happier place and that this transformation is one of Spiritism's most important goals.

8.　　That we should all do everything we can to disseminate the Spiritist revelation, which will greatly accelerate the transformation of our planet into a world dedicated only to regeneration.

9. That even the most unexpected deaths - when young people leave the earth before their elders, for example (a circumstance considered so cruel and senseless by so many) - occur for the most perfect of reasons, exclusively to foster growth and regeneration.

10.　　That many times these premature deaths are a great blessing because they help these individuals to avoid falling into certain temptations of earthly life, which might otherwise have been very detrimental to them if they had remained in this world any longer.

11.　That when a human spirit discarnates they go on following their spiritual path, and that, even in the 'afterlife' it can look forward to wonderful things in its future.

12.　　That those who have discarnated are living alongside us, quite close to us, that they surround and protects us, and that they are always happy to feel our positive thoughts about them.

13.　That to wish a good man a long stay on earth is like wishing that a prisoner be kept in jail even after his sentence is served; and that to wish a cruel man a quick death is like wanting to free a criminal from prison before even half his sentence has been served.

14.　　That to a spirit, real freedom is freedom from material attachments so living on earth is like being in prison. That, in fact, considering that earthly life is no more than a moment in eternity, a passing phase in a spirit's eternal succession lives; only spiritual life can be considered real.

15.   That it would be possible for a person to find happiness on earth if one would only look for it in the pleasures of spiritual life, which is eternal, instead of continuously frustrating oneself by seeking it in the fleeting pleasures of material existence.

16.   That anyone who has managed to be content with what one has, has saved oneself considerable suffering. Simply by observing those who have less, a human being can feel rich by comparison and free oneself false needs that might otherwise ruin one's happiness.

17.   That it is often the case that an initially unfortunate event becomes a springboard for a whole series of very fortunate ones; while, by the same token, there are circumstances that seem to be lucky, which ultimately cause tragic events.

18.   That everything that seems unfortunate from an earthly perspective ends with corporeal existence and is then seen from a very different perspective from spiritual life and that human beings create their most unpleasant circumstances by seeking happiness in unbridled pleasure, material turmoil, senseless commotion, and the satisfaction of human vanity. These pursuits sum up the stuff of hell on earth; they are the temptations that most confound humanity.

19.   That Spiritism makes all of these truths so clear and straightforward that they are beyond question. Through this added understanding, Spiritism allows us to see for ourselves that it is worth to be patient through the loss of material wealth or even bodily health during our daily battles through earthly existence. It is inestimably worth if through these losses and this patience we gain a glorious life beyond this one.

20.   That, it's not uncommon for a person in active pursuit of spiritual happiness to feel almost exhausted from one's efforts to liberate oneself from the temptations of physical pleasure and become discouraged. Sometimes, indeed quite often, such a spirit will mistakenly assume that one's

efforts have been useless, multiplying one's fatigue by adding to it a measure of despondency.

21. That we should wait patiently for the moment of our liberation from material existence. We must remember that we have important tasks and missions to complete during our earthly lives and responsibilities to live up to that, once dealt with, can lead us back to a reunion with our loved ones who wait for us even now, in a spiritual realm.

22. That some of the problems we go through are put in place to test and exercise our intellect as much as to develop our patience and resignation and that everyone can and should overcome them. That it's important to try to suffer without complaint, but it is also important to go on fighting even when our best efforts fail without ever losing hope no matter what.

23. That there is only merit in sacrificing ourselves when we do it for others. To freely choose to sacrifice our physical bodies for any other reason constitutes a kind of suicide.

24. That we should not just stand by and watch while collective trials occur nearby or ignore its victims if they are within reach. If God placed us that near people in pain, it is because we are meant to help them through their pain or attenuate as much as possible by using whatever means we have at our disposal.

25. That a spiritist should never willingly act as an instrument of torture or, for that matter, cause suffering to one's fellow being in any way; rather, one should work tirelessly to alleviate pain, knowing that, whatever one does, in the end the will of God will prevail.

26. That, although we are all here for the sake of redeeming ourselves first and foremost, if we wish to live by the divine law of Love and Charity, without which there is no salvation, we must also make every attempt to soften the hardship other people are going through for the sake of their redemption.

27. That we should not help the dying to leave this earth more quickly because only God knows when each one of

us should die and that, in fact, the final moments of someone's life can help them repent and choose a better path so the right thing to do is to alleviate the pain of anyone who is near death in any way possible, but always - at any cost - avoid the risk of cutting off one's life.

28.   That the hardships we live through can represent gains for others, both morally and materially.   In fact, some sacrifices we make not only help others directly, but also serve as good examples for them.   And a good example can bring those in pain both the resignation and the hope for the future they so sorely need.

CHAPTER 6
CHRIST THE CONSOLER

The gentle yoke

"Come to me, all you who are weary and burdened, and I will give you rest. Take my yoke upon you and learn from me, for I am gentle and humble in heart, and you will find rest for your souls. For my yoke is easy and my burden is light." (Matthew, chapter 11: 28-30)

Jesus promised that those who trusted him and took his words to heart would see their hardships grow softer and, in future, be consoled. The same could not be said, however, for those who would not believe and expect another life to greet them after death, or had doubts about the hereafter. For these people, nothing can lessen life's afflictions, for only faith in life after death can really console us when our problems on earth start to feel unbearable and seem insoluble.

The promised consoler

"If you love me, you will obey what I command. And I will ask the Father, and he will give you another Counselor to be with you forever— the Spirit of truth. The world cannot accept him, because it neither sees him nor knows him. But you know him, for he lives with you and will be in you. But the Counselor, the Holy Spirit, whom the Father will send in my name, will teach you all things and will remind you of everything I have said to you. (John, chapter 14: 15-17 and 26)

In this famous passage, Jesus promised another consoler, The Spirit of Truth, (who brought us Spiritism). Spiritism came to teach us many things (since in Jesus' time it wasn't possible to say everything because of the still rudimentary level of spiritual evolution attained by the people of that time). It also came to remind us of what Christ himself had taught, explaining, in a more straightforward way, what Jesus had had to tell us through parables and symbols.

Spiritism came, then, to clarify many mysteries and bring comfort to those who suffer by showing them that there is a logical explanation for their suffering, even if it has to be sought in their past lives.

Spiritism also explains the purpose of suffering. Suffering, Spiritism tells us, comes to us fundamentally for our own good. It comes to ensure our happiness in future existences. Also, Spiritism helps humanity understand that since everything that is suffered is necessary and deserved no suffering is either pointless or unjust.

By believing in the truths imparted or interpreted by Spiritism, a human being can come to know a kind of faith that can better help oneself bear the burdens of life, for one comes to understand that these burdens are, in fact, minor problems and the certainty of future happiness helps the person to develop both patience and resignation.

In this chapter, the spirits teach:

1. That we should always return to the path of benevolence, which is the only one that can lead to real life (spiritual life).

2. That all of us, whether incarnate or discarnate, should help one another.

3. That death doesn't exist and that material life is no more than a test of our progress.

4. That we should love one another first and foremost and, second only to that, educate ourselves in Christianity, for all truths can be found there (apparent errors are due exclusively to human misinterpretations).

5. That those who suffer should accept their pain because they will also receive consolation; and that they should always pick up their work wherever they left off the day before without a doubt in their minds that the Spirit of Truth (Jesus) watches over us all.

6. That the weariness and suffering we are now experiencing are temporary and always eventually followed by great joys, which we will all experience in future.

7. That God smiles upon those who, though suffering themselves, rise to the occasion when necessary in order to help those in greater need.

8. That everyone should understand the purpose of human trials and not envy the rich, for they are often going through even more dangerous trials than those who might think they have cause to envy them.

9. That Jesus is the greatest healer of souls, always ready with just the right medicine for each of us. And that the weak, the suffering, and the ill are his favorite children.

10. That Spiritism is an inspiring invitation to us, the human family, to rise and recover from the moral illnesses from which we suffer, removing impiety, lies, errors and doubt from our lives.

11. That two attitudes must be especially developed by those who wish to evolve: abnegation, which is the practice of benevolence without desire to profit by it, and devotion, which is the effort to be benevolent without fail; for these virtues, in combination, strengthen the soul as nothing else can; together they contain all the duties that charity and humility demand of us.

CHAPTER 7

BLESSED ARE THE POOR IN SPIRIT

What does "poor in spirit" mean?

Blessed are the poor in spirit, for theirs is the kingdom of heaven. (Matthew, chapter 5: 3)

Many were confused about whom Jesus had in mind when he referred to the "poor in spirit". He did not mean to imply that they were unintelligent; rather, he was talking about those who were humble enough to have a special place reserved for them in Spirituality (the hereafter).

Generally speaking in our world, knowledgeable men and women consider themselves so erudite that believing in God, or anything spiritual for that matter, would be beneath them; such things are considered too childish to deserve serious attention. In fact, some go so far as to believe themselves so all knowing that they can deny the existence of God because anything in this world can be explained by their sciences without recourse to God.

Ironically, by refusing to accept the fact that there is an intelligence and scope of action vastly larger than their own - God's universal intelligence - they sabotage the process of their own intellectual progress as well as the expansion of the knowledge they so prize. Because they cannot accept that anything can happen beyond their vision or scope of action, they cannot accept the existence of invisible worlds. And they're so convinced of their own wisdom that it is quite beyond them to conceive of rewards reserved exclusively for those who are "poor in spirit" and, unlike themselves, humble. But no matter, one day even these will reach a level discernment that will allow them to move on. Finally they will understand and admit that what they had refused to believe is true.

When Jesus said, "The Kingdom of Heaven belongs to the simple" he meant that in order to enter Spiritual Life on good terms, a person must cultivate simplicity of heart and humility of spirit. He also wanted to make it very clear that, as long as a person has just two special qualities: simplicity and humility, even an ignorant person will have a better chance to do well and prosper in the Spirit World than a knowledgeable individual who thinks oneself cleverer than God. Jesus thinks of humility as a virtue that brings people closer to God and pride as a vice that tears them further and further from Him, for humility leads to submission to God whereas pride fuels rebellion against Him.

He who exalts himself shall be humbled

At that time the disciples came to Jesus and asked, "Who is the greatest in the kingdom of heaven?" He called a little child and had him stand among them. And he said: "I tell you the truth, unless you change and become like little children, you will never enter the kingdom of heaven. Therefore, whoever humbles himself like this child is the greatest in the kingdom of heaven. And whoever welcomes a little child like this in my name welcomes me." (Matthew, chapter 18: 1-5)

Then the mother of Zebedee's sons came to Jesus with her sons and, kneeling down, asked a favor of him. "What is it you want?" he asked. She said, "Grant that one of these two sons of mine may sit at your right and the other at your left in your kingdom." "You don't know what you are asking," Jesus said to them. "Can you drink the cup I am going to drink?" "We can," they answered. Jesus said to them, "You will indeed drink from my cup, but to sit at my right or left is not for me to grant. These places belong to those for whom they have been prepared by my Father."

When the ten heard about this, they were indignant with the two brothers. Jesus called them together and said, "You know that the rulers of the Gentiles lord it over them, and their high officials exercise authority over them. Not so with you. Instead, whoever wants to become great among you must be your servant, and whoever wants to be first must be your slave— just as the Son of Man did not come to be served, but to serve, and to give his life as a ransom for many." (Matthew, chapter 20: 20-28)

One Sabbath, when Jesus went to eat in the house of a prominent Pharisee, he was being carefully watched. When he noticed how the guests picked the places of honor at the table, he told them this parable: "When someone invites you to a wedding feast, do not take the place of honor, for a person more distinguished than you may have been invited. If so, the host who invited both of you will come and say to you, 'Give this man your seat.' Then, humiliated, you will have to take the least important place. But when you are invited, take the lowest place, so that when your host comes, he will say to you, 'Friend, move up to a better place.' Then you will be honored in the presence of all your fellow guests. For everyone who exalts himself will be humbled, and he who humbles himself will be exalted." (Luke, chapter 14: 1 and 7-11)

The evangelists used these texts to exalt the principle of humility, which, as Jesus had said, is essential to anyone who yearns for happiness in the hereafter. As an example, Jesus pointed to a child, to illustrate the fact that to reach the kingdom of heaven, a person must be like a child in terms of not feeling superior to anyone or infallible. Jesus then summarized everything with the aphorism, "For everyone who exalts himself will be humbled and he who humbles himself will be exalted."

Spiritism shows us that those who occupied highly important positions in earthly life often find themselves in sharply reduced circumstances in the spirit world. On the other hand, many who did not have important positions on earth, but spent their time cultivating spiritual virtues, find themselves occupying very comfortable positions there. By the same token, Spiritism demonstrates the fact that some people, who were dominated by pride and ambition when they occupied positions of influence in a particular earthly life, end up having to live in humbling circumstances during a future incarnation.

Jesus counsels us, therefore, to avoid positions of great power in relation to other human beings in favor of keeping ourselves in a modest position, for our merit and effort will always be rewarded.

Mysteries are hidden from the learned and prudent

> At that time Jesus said, "I praise you, Father, Lord of heaven and earth, because you have hidden these things from the wise and learned, and revealed them to little children. Yes, Father, for this was your good pleasure. (Matthew, chapter 11: 25)

Small, simple children represent those who are humble and would never consider themselves greater than God or even superior to other human beings... it is to these that God reveals heavenly secrets, none other than the secrets of the spiritual world; He leaves the study of earthly secrets to the learned and prudent (meaning the proud, who sometimes deny the existence of God or impudently treat Him as an equal). Spirits do not submit to their will or demands because while God listens lovingly to those who seek Him with humility in their hearts, He does not hear those who come to Him with demands as if their stature were greater than His own.

A lot of people wonder why God does not produce fantastic metaphysical phenomena to convince unbelievers to have faith. He could simply create a display so amazing that multitudes would see and talk about, couldn't He? Well, of course, He could. But if He did that what merit would there be in the faith of these new believers? Would they have invested anything of themselves in this newfound faith? What about the leap of faith that would have allowed them to discover God for themselves?

Besides, there are people for whom no amount of proof is enough. They might witness extraordinary demonstrations and deny what they had seen with their own eyes rather than accept as real something that doesn't fit their worldview. They let their pride hold back their spiritual (both moral and intellectual) evolution. There's nothing anyone can do but wait

64

for him or her to mature in his or her own time. But God abandons no one; He waits for us each to heal our pride in our own time and when we are finally ready to look for Him, we find him right there just where He's always been, inside us, waiting for us to step into His wide open arms like children...

In this chapter the spirits teach:

1. That humility - a much-ignored virtue - is essential in order for people to behave like equals and, as such, help one another.

2. That pride is the enemy of humility.

3. That the bodies of the rich are no different from those of the poor; both are made of the same divine substance. Also, that today's rich individual can have been just as poor in a previous incarnation as the homeless person one now despises, and that, in any case, all material wealth disappears with the death of the body.

4. That in the eyes of God all people are equal; the only differences He sees among them are in the virtues they possess.

5. That all spirits are made of the same essence and incarnate in bodies of the same kind.

6. That it would be foolish for the poor to envy the excessive wealth some choose to flaunt (in many cases it is preferable to be poor and have humility than to have all the wealth in the world and have to endure all the pain that so often accompanies it).

7. That, since no one is completely innocent, those who suffer injustices should be tolerant of their oppressors and suffer with resignation through the humiliations that have come to them as trials or as opportunities for purification.

8. That pride (along with selfishness) is the root of all evil, not money; pride is responsible for all the suffering and general malaise there is on earth.

9. That God punishes the vain; He lets them advance for a while, giving them time to think about what they are doing, but sooner or later their ordeals will come.

10. That no one should be proud of one's own intelligence for if God gave him or her the opportunity to be intelligent, it is because He wanted that intelligence to be used for the common good.

CHAPTER 8

BLESSED ARE THE PURE IN HEART

Simplicity and pureness of heart

Blessed are the pure in heart, for they will see God. (Matthew, chapter 5: 8)

People were bringing little children to Jesus to have him touch them, but the disciples rebuked them. When Jesus saw this, he was indignant. He said to them, "Let the little children come to me, and do not hinder them, for the kingdom of God belongs to such as these. I tell you the truth, anyone who will not receive the kingdom of God like a little child will never enter it." And he took the children in his arms, put his hands on them and blessed them. (Mark, chapter 10: 13-16)

Purity of heart represents simplicity and humility, the opposite of pride and selfishness. That's why Jesus used little children as examples of purity. Childhood is a moment when a reincarnated spirit, hasn't yet had a chance to feel or manifest bad tendencies it may have brought with it from other lives. As such, childhood is the perfect opportunity to educate a spirit so that the bad habits that may lie dormant within oneself can be changed. Besides that, childhood represents an image of innocence and candor. Jesus did not say that the kingdom of heaven was for children, but for those who were like children.

Before incarnating, the spirit goes through a period during which it feels disoriented and, following that, it undergoes a trance state very much like sleep. During this period of somnolence the incarnating spirit forgets its past in order to prepare itself for a new experience on earth. Everything, which might otherwise have disturbed it, is forgotten. After it is born the spirit will gradually develop and, little by little, certain memories will return; but for the first few years the incarnated spirit will be a child so the character and ways of being it acquired in other lives will still be locked in sleep. That's why childhood is the best time to educate an incarnated spirit. When a child is reached during this stage there is a much better chance for him to change certain harmful tendencies from his past in order to progress more quickly through the lifetime that is just beginning.

Sinning by means of thought: Adultery

> *"You have heard that it was said, 'Do not commit adultery.' But I tell you that anyone who looks at a woman lustfully has already committed adultery with her in his heart. (Matthew, chapter 5: 27 and 28)*

Jesus used the term "adultery" in a larger sense, meaning evil or sin. He was against any kind of malevolence, even in thought, because it constituted a sign of imperfection. As a soul evolves, it tries to progress even if only very gradually. The spirits who are already able to avoid both dark deeds and dark thoughts have progressed enormously. Others, who may still think of behaving in ways that would hurt those around them, but manage to resist the temptation and to act on their thoughts, have also made progress. But finally, there are those who not only imagine wrong deeds but also, unfortunately, follow through and practice them. This group of spirits has long arduous journeys ahead of it.

True pureness – Unwashed hands

> *Then some Pharisees and teachers of the law came to Jesus from Jerusalem and asked, "Why do your disciples break the tradition of the elders? They don't wash their hands before they eat!" Jesus replied, "And why do you break the command of God for the sake of your tradition? For God said, 'Honor your father and mother' and 'anyone who curses his father or mother must be put to death.' But you say that if a man says to his father or mother, 'Whatever help you might otherwise have received from me is a gift*

devoted to God,' he is not to 'honor his father' with it. Thus you nullify the word of God for the sake of your tradition. You hypocrites! Isaiah was right when he prophesied about you:' These people honor me with their lips, but their hearts are far from me. They worship me in vain; their teachings are but rules taught by men.'" Jesus called the crowd to him and said, "Listen and understand. What goes into a man's mouth does not make him 'unclean,' but what comes out of his mouth, that is what makes him 'unclean.'" Then the disciples came to him and asked, "Do you know that the Pharisees were offended when they heard this?" He replied, "Every plant that my heavenly Father has not planted will be pulled up by the roots. Leave them; they are blind guides. If a blind man leads a blind man, both will fall into a pit." Peter said, "Explain the parable to us." "Are you still so dull?" Jesus asked them. "Don't you see that whatever enters the mouth goes into the stomach and then out of the body? But the things that come out of the mouth come from the heart, and these make a man 'unclean.' For out of the heart come evil thoughts, murder, adultery, sexual immorality, theft, false testimony, slander. These are what make a man 'unclean'; but eating with unwashed hands does not make him 'unclean.' "
(Matthew, chapter 15: 1-20)

When Jesus had finished speaking, a Pharisee invited him to eat with him; so he went in and reclined at the table. But the Pharisee, noticing that Jesus did not first wash before the meal, was surprised. Then the Lord said to him, "Now then, you Pharisees clean the outside of the cup and dish, but inside you are full of greed and wickedness. You foolish people! Did not the one who made the outside make the inside also? (Luke, chapter 11: 37-40)

As years went by, the Jews gradually forgot the true commandments and began to cultivate more superficial practices, various rituals and rules that prioritized the external and formal over the internal or essential. For example, although they were very concerned about the cleanliness of their hands, they cared little about keeping their feelings pure.

With time they grew used to thinking that God required no more of them than the cleanliness of their hands. After the birth of Christianity, the same thing started happening. People started paying more attention to outer forms like rituals, ceremonies and material symbols than to matters of the heart and mind (spiritual matters). The purpose of religion is to lead the human beings back to God, which is not something that can be accomplished through superficial, external practices, but rather through personal effort to become a better person by cultivating purity of heart.

Offences – If your hand be the cause of an offence, cut it off.

> But if anyone causes one of these little ones who believe in me to sin, it would be better for him to have a large millstone hung around his neck and to be drowned in the depths of the sea. "Woe to the world because of the things that cause people to sin! Such things must come, but woe to the man through whom they come! If your hand or your foot causes you to sin, cut it off and throw it away. It is better for you to enter life maimed or crippled than to have two hands or two feet and be thrown into eternal fire. And if your eye causes you to sin, gouge it out and throw it away. It is better for you to enter life with one eye than to have two eyes and be thrown into the fire of hell. (Matthew, chapter 18: 6-9; Matthew, chapter 5: 29-30)

The term "offence", as used by Jesus referred to the result of a morally unjustifiable action or, in other words, everything that resulted from human vices and imperfections. In this sense, when Jesus said *"Such things must come, but woe to the man through whom they come!* He meant that, given the fact that men and women were imperfect, offences would naturally occur. In addition, he was also referring to the fact that the earth is still a planet of tests and atonements with people hurting one another for the problems they had provoked. In this way, by providing just punishment, that is, something apparently wrong (or evil) can come to cause a valuable change; this is one of the most important ways in which evolution works.

In more evolved worlds, where evil no longer exists, everyone does the right thing and there is no need for what Jesus called sins or offences. When Jesus said, *woe to the man through whom they come!* He meant that, although offences (wrongs done to others) can act as ways to fulfill Divine Laws (by providing opportunities for atonement to those who need it) that does not mean the person who created the offence would not have to suffer for it. One may have been an instrument of divine law in meting out necessary atonement, but the act of producing the offence was morally wrong so, as the person who unleashed the offence, one will have to atone.

When Jesus said, *if your hand causes you to sin, cut it off*, he meant that when we notice an impure thought or feeling inside us, we should do everything possible to expel this feeling. Clearly, Jesus did not mean that we should mutilate our bodies; this image, which Christ used, cannot be taken literally.

In this chapter the spirits teach:

1. That Jesus' words were not merely an invitation to children, but rather, they represented a call to the spiritual children of the planet: the weak, the addicted, the enslaved, the sinners.

2. That Jesus wanted this category of unhappy creatures to look for him for help with the same tender trust that children feel when they go to parents or teachers.

3. That Jesus was the real founder of Spiritism, which with its logic will attract not only the small children but also people of good will.

4. That we have the best thing there is, which is love, a virtue that cannot deteriorate like material things.

5. That when looking for a cure for one's body, one should ask, before anything else, for a cure for one's soul.

In this chapter Kardec teaches:

1. That when hardship is not the result of any action in one's current life, it is probably the result of one's actions in past lives.

2. That many things that we think happen by chance (or as a result of bad luck) are actually aligned with the Laws of God, and therefore neither arbitrary nor unjust; and that every time someone is punished, it is because he has made some kind of mistake which warranted that punishment, either in this life or a past one.

CHAPTER 9

BLESSED ARE THE MEEK AND THE PEACEMAKER

Insults and violence

Blessed are the meek, for they will inherit the earth. (Matthew, chapter 5: 5)

Blessed are the peacemakers, for they will be called sons of God. (Matthew, chapter 5: 9)

"You have heard that it was said to the people long ago, 'Do not murder, and anyone who murders will be subject to judgment.' But I tell you that anyone who is angry with his brother will be subject to judgment. Again, anyone who says to his brother, 'Raca, ' is answerable to the Sanhedrin. But anyone who says, 'You fool!' will be in danger of the fire of hell. (Matthew, chapter 5: 21-22)

Through these words, Jesus condemned violence, anger and any aggressive action toward others. The word *Raca*, to the Hebrews, was a term of scorn that meant a *worthless person*, and it was said while spitting and turning one's head to the side. Jesus tried to show that every rude word represented a feeling against love and sense of charity that should be the basis of the relationship among human beings.

After the humility before God, Jesus recommended the charity and brotherhood with others. On the other hand, while Jesus preached the renunciation of the world's goods, he said "the meek shall inherit the earth in the future." But one thing is not the opposite of the other, although it may seem at first sight.

The explanation is that, at this moment, the material goods are owned by the violent and unethical people to the damage of the good and peaceful ones, but humanity moves toward progress. So, in the future, when the earth is in another class of world, the bad will no longer own material goods, because it could no longer live in a world that has reached better levels of evolution. Then the meek and peacemaker will certainly be, owners of world's goods, which will not be used with selfishness.

In this chapter the spirits teach:

1. That we should strive to be the same in all situations, both in society and in intimacy, once, by appearance we can fool people, but we can never deceive God.

2. That we should exercise the virtue of patience, since suffering is a blessing that God sends us to correct our past sins.

3. That the easier way of doing charity is to give alms to the poor, but there is another kind of love, the more difficult and worthwhile, which is the act of forgiving those who God has placed in our path as an instrument of suffering as well as a way for us to exercise our patience.

4. That obedience, in the view of spirituality, is always accompanied by a reason (not being a blind obedience), and resignation comes with the support of feeling, without pretense, pride or selfishness.

5. That we must not be overcome by laziness and that we must always move forward, based on the new teachings that are brought by Spiritism.

6. That the choleric (or angry) is unfortunate and makes unhappy all the people who live with him or her, that anger impairs health; the spiritist must seek to prevent the cultivation of cholera, which is contrary to charity and Christian humility.

7. That the idea that an individual is unable to change its very nature is false; that one only continues with vices and imperfections if one wants to, because if one wishes, one can always correct them, and if it were not so, the law of progress wouldn't exist.

CHAPTER 10

BLESSED ARE THE MERCIFUL

Forgive others so that God may forgive you

Blessed are the merciful, for they will be shown mercy. (Matthew, chapter 5: 7)

For if you forgive men when they sin against you, your heavenly Father will also forgive you. But if you do not forgive men their sins, your Father will not forgive your sins. (Matthew, chapter 6: 14-15)

If your brother sins against you, go and show him his fault, just between the two of you. If he listens to you, you have won your brother over. Then Peter came to Jesus and asked, "Lord, how many times shall I forgive my brother when he sins against me? Up to seven times?" Jesus answered, "I tell you, not seven times, but seventy-seven times. (Matthew, chapter 18: 15, 21-22)

Mercy is the forgetting and forgiving of sins. These attitudes are characteristic of evolved souls, and Jesus recommends that mercy should have no boundaries when he says to forgive "seventy times seven." But there are two ways to forgive: the first is true, generous, gentle, and avoids hurting the self-esteem of the opponent; the second imposes conditions for forgiveness. In the latter case there is no generosity, but only a way to satisfy the pride of the one who is said offended. The one who acts in a more conciliatory and disinterested way has more greatness in soul and always wins the sympathy of people.

Reconciliation with your adversaries

Settle matters quickly with your adversary who is taking you to court. Do it while you are still with him on the way, or he may hand you over to the judge, and the judge may hand you over to the officer, and you may be thrown into prison. I tell you the truth; you will not get out until you have paid the last penny. (Matthew, chapter 5: 25-26)

Death doesn't free us from our opponents. Revengeful spirits chase, even after discarnation, those that had been their enemies during their lives. Many times the evil spirit wait for its opponents to reincarnate in order to easily reach and torment them, bringing out obsessions, subjugation and possessions. The latter are, mostly, victims of chasing due to an unfortunate act that had been done in a previous life.

That's why it is important that the person may as soon as possible fix the evils one has caused to others and forgives one's enemies, thus avoiding suffering in some future incarnation. Certainly believing that God and the laws of life do not allow anyone to suffer without reason or anyone who has sincerely forgiven to become victim of aggression out of any reason.

The sacrifice most agreeable to God

"Therefore, if you are offering your gift at the altar and there remember that your brother has something against you, leave your gift there in front of the altar. First go and be reconciled to your brother; then come and offer your gift. (Matthew, chapter 5: 23-24)

Before presenting themselves before God, one must first forgive one's opponent. The Jews, by the time Jesus lived, were used to make offerings, and Jesus used this fact as a kind of image to be followed by the good person. In other words, to report to the temple of the Lord, the believer must leave any bad feeling behind, such as hatred, hostility or aggression against the fellow.

The speck and the beam in the eye

Why do you look at the speck of sawdust in your brother's eye and pay no attention to the plank in your own eye? How can you say to your brother, 'Let me take the speck out of your eye,' when all the time there is a plank in your own eye? You hypocrite, first take the plank out of your own eye, and then you will see clearly to remove the speck from your brother's eye. (Matthew, chapter 7: 3-5)

Pride is the main obstacle for the progress of the spirit. It's the center from which many other human's faults can come out of. Pride, in addition, makes people see the evil in others and not within them. This feeling is contradictory and opposes charity. That's why Jesus so many times had advised us to fight the pride.

Do not judge others if you do not wish to be judged in return – he that is without a sin let him be the first to cast a stone

"Do not judge, or you too will be judged. For in the same way you judge others, you will be judged, and with the measure you use, it will be measured to you. (Matthew, chapter 7: 1, 2)

The teachers of the law and the Pharisees brought in a woman caught in adultery. They made her stand before the group and said to Jesus, "Teacher, this woman was caught in the act of adultery. In the Law Moses commanded us to stone such women. Now what do you say?" They were using this question as a trap, in order to have a basis for accusing him. But Jesus bent down and started to write on the ground with his finger. When they kept on questioning him, he straightened up and said to them, "If any one of you is without sin, let him be the first to throw a stone at her." Again he stooped down and wrote on the ground. At this, those who heard began to go away one at a time, the older ones first, until only Jesus was left, with the woman still standing there. Jesus straightened up and asked her, "Woman, where are they? Has no one condemned you?" "No one, sir," she said. "Then neither do I condemn you," Jesus declared. "Go now and leave your life of sin." (John, chapter 8: 3-11)

When Jesus recommended being the first to throw a stone the one who is without sin, he recommended us to be indulgent. That means we shouldn't be harder on others than we are on ourselves. Disapproving someone's behavior should hold two objectives: one, admirable, which is to repress the evil; the other, unacceptable, which is making the person who we are criticizing disbelieved. The authority to call someone's attention should come from the moral authority of the person who is censuring. Genuine authority can only be found on the example of the person's practicing the good.

In this chapter, the spirits teach:

1. That we must forgive not seven times, but seventy times seven times (in other words, we must forgive without limits, be gentle and humble from the heart, this way we become invulnerable to attacks and misdeeds).

2. That this concept must be divulged and cultivated by the spiritists, that forgiveness should not happen in words only, but especially through acts.

3. That forgiving the enemies is giving them a proof of friendship.

4. That if we were more indulgent and serene, many happenings that result in conflicts would have been easily forgotten.

5. That there is forgiveness with words and forgiveness from the heart, and the only worthy one is those that come from the heart, once God isn't pleased with appearances.

6. That the complete and absolute forgetting of the offenses is a characteristic of the great spirits, and the true forgiveness is known by acts more than by words.

7. That indulgence is a feeling that doesn't see any faults in others or avoids talking about them. Indulgence doesn't waste time with other people's bad acts and neither censures them. It only gives advice, mostly softly. We should be hard on ourselves and indulgent with our fellow beings.

8. That God, at the last level, is who judges us and sees the personal thoughts of each of us.

9. That we must be indulgent, because the indulgence attracts and calms, while the strictness disheartens, pushes away and irritates.

10. That when we forgive others, we should not only forget the offences, but also try to send them love, which has a purifying action.

11. That we should practice charity, whose character is modesty and humility.

12. That when we reprimand others, we should do it moderately, with a noble purpose, never to put them down. If repression has a noble intention, it is desirable, because this is a good and a must that charity recommends; but in order to reprimand someone, we should first think if we don't deserve to be reprimanded either.

13. That it is wrong to censure someone by putting him or her down in front of others, but if we do care about preserving the person, by not making the reprimand public, the warning will be worth for him or her, and useful for his or her improvement.

14. If a person's faults are harming oneself, there is no use in announcing them, but if it can harm others, revealing them may become a must.

CHAPTER 11

LOVE YOUR NEIGHBOR AS YOURSELF

Hearing that Jesus had silenced the Sadducees, the Pharisees got together. One of them, an expert in the law, tested him with this question: "Teacher, which is the greatest commandment in the Law?" Jesus replied: " 'Love the Lord your God with all your heart and with all your soul and with all your mind.' This is the first and greatest commandment. And the second is like it: 'Love your neighbor as yourself.' All the Law and the Prophets hang on these two commandments." (Matthew, chapter, 22: 34-40)

So in everything, do to others what you would have them do to you, for this sums up the Law and the Prophets. (Matthew, chapter, 7: 12)

Do to others, as you would have them do to you. (Luke, chapter 6: 31)

"Therefore, the kingdom of heaven is like a king who wanted to settle accounts with his servants. As he began the settlement, a man who owed him ten thousand talents was brought to him. Since he was not able to pay, the master ordered that he and his wife and his children and all that he had be sold to repay the debt. "The servant fell on his knees before him. 'Be patient with me,' he begged, 'and I will pay back everything.' The servant's master took pity on him, canceled the debt and let him go. "But when that servant went out, he found one of his fellow servants who owed him a hundred denarii. He grabbed him and began to choke him. 'Pay back what you owe me!' he demanded. "His fellow servant fell to his knees and begged him, 'Be patient with me, and I will pay you back.' "But he refused. Instead, he went off and had the man thrown into prison until he could pay the debt. When the other servants saw what had happened, they were greatly distressed and went and told their master everything that had happened. "Then the master called the servant in. 'You wicked servant,' he said, 'I canceled all that debt of yours because you begged me to.

> *Shouldn't you have had mercy on your fellow servant just as I had on you?' In anger his master turned him over to the jailers to be tortured, until he should pay back all he owed. "This is how my heavenly Father will treat each of you unless you forgive your brother from your heart." (Matthew, chapter 18: 23-35)*

"To love your neighbor as yourself and to do to others as you would have them do to you," expresses the most complete form of charity and it is a practice that tends to eliminate selfishness. When these practices have been adopted as a rule of conduct and as the base of all institutions, then the human beings will understand true fraternity and so make it possible for peace and justice to reign on this planet.

Give to Caesar that which belongs to Caesar

> *When the Pharisees went out and laid plans to trap him in his words. They sent their disciples to him along with the Herodians. "Teacher," they said, "we know you are a man of integrity and that you teach the way of God in accordance with the truth. You aren't swayed by men, because you pay no attention to who they are. Tell us then, what is your opinion? Is it right to pay taxes to Caesar or not?" But Jesus, knowing their evil intent, said, "You hypocrites, why are you trying to trap me? Show me the coin used for paying the tax." They brought him a denarius, and he asked them, "Whose portrait is this? And whose inscription?" "Caesar's," they replied. Then he said to them, "Give to Caesar what is Caesar's, and to God what is God's." When they heard this, they were amazed. So they left him and went away. (Matthew, chapter 22: 15-22; Mark, chapter 12: 13-17)*

The Jews were against paying tributes to the Romans, and this payment became a religious question. With this question they tried to set a trap to Jesus depending on the answer he was going to give (if the reply was against the payment of the tribute, Jesus, as a result, would be placing himself against the Emperor). But Jesus, who understood the malice of the inquirers, got around this difficulty and replied: "Give to Caesar what is Caesar's;" with that Jesus was teaching us to give to each one what was due to them.

In this chapter, the spirits teach:

1. That love summarizes Jesus' doctrine as a whole.

2. That a person has only instincts within one's origins, as one advances one has sensations and, finally, as one evolves, one shows one's feelings.

3. That the main feeling is love that can end with social miseries.

4. That reincarnation provides victory over death.

5. That a person must defeat one's instincts, as to consolidate feelings, by enhancing them and overcoming the matter; that instincts are the embryos of the feelings and that less advanced beings are the ones who are found attached to instincts.

6. That the spirits must be cared, and the future wealth depends on the current effort.

7. That human beings should understand and practice the law of love; that God had put love in all humans, and this love grows along with morality and intelligence that the individual develops.

8. That love ends up to be the source that generates sincere and long affections, so as the human beings face the hard chores of life.

9. That the law of love points out that the human beings may triumph over individual selfishness, family, caste and nationality; there shouldn't be limits or frontiers for love, once it must involve the entire humanity.

10. That the law of love will bring out all of our moral improvement and the joy during our terrestrial life, and if we love each other, soon earth will be transformed.

11. That selfishness stops moral progress from happening on earth, and that Spiritism had arisen with the task of banishing terrestrial selfishness (the greatest barrier to a person's happiness).

12. That it regards to all Spiritists the effort of eliminating selfishness from earth, as so it can arise in the worlds' scale. But first of all it is necessary that everyone eliminate it from one's own heart.

13. That selfishness is charity denial and that without charity there will be neither rest nor safety to human society.

14. That God created us for eternal happiness, but that the earth's individual can be happy if one searches happiness on goodness, and not on material pleasures.

15. That charity is attained through forgiveness towards criminals, since they repent their faults, in the same way we must regret ours.

16. That charity is not only the giving or consoling, but also benevolence towards our fellow beings.

17. That the time for brotherhood among earth's inhabitants is closer.

18. That very soon the rebelled and inferior spirits will go to inferior worlds, according to its tendencies.

Return goodness for evil

"You have heard that it was said, 'Love your neighbor and hate your enemy.' But I tell you: Love your enemies and pray for those who persecute you, that you may be sons of your Father in heaven. He causes his sun to rise on the evil and the good, and sends rain on the righteous and the unrighteous. If you love those who love you, what reward will you get? Are not even the tax collectors doing that? And if you greet only your brothers, what are you doing more than others? Do not even pagans do that? (Matthew, chapter 5: 43-47)

For I tell you that unless your righteousness surpasses that of the Pharisees and the teachers of the law, you will certainly not enter the kingdom of heaven. (Matthew, chapter 5: 20)

If you love those who love you, what credit is that to you? Even 'sinners' love those who love them. And if you do good to those who are good to you, what credit is that to you? Even 'sinners' do that. And if you lend to those from whom you expect repayment, what credit is that to you? Even 'sinners' lend to 'sinners,' expecting to be repaid in full. But love your enemies, do good to them, and lend to them without expecting to get anything back. Then your reward will be great, and you will be sons of the Most High, because he is kind to the ungrateful and wicked. Be merciful, just as your Father is merciful. (Luke, chapter 6: 32-36)

Love toward our neighbors holds the principle of charity and the love to the enemy represents one of the greatest victories over our pride and selfishness. Yet, Jesus didn't intend that the term "love" your enemies meant the same feeling that one has toward one's brother or friend. After all, this feeling is based on trust and it isn't reasonable to trust someone who doesn't want us good. Nobody can have equal feelings for a friend and for a great opponent. And there is a physical explanation for that: bad thoughts cause negative impression, and bring unpleasant sensations; good thoughts bring pleasant sensations. It's natural that there are some differences in sensations we have toward a friend or an enemy.

To love enemies means love them in a different way from the way you love your friends. The word is the same (love), but there is a difference in both cases. To love the enemies, therefore is, not having the same affection you have for a friend, which is naturally impossible, but not bearing bad feelings toward them such as hate, sorrow or desire for revenge. It is forgiving them under any conditions, accepting a future possibility of reconciliation, wishing them good, feeling joy for the good things that may happen to them, providing help whenever they need it. It is not harming them either with words or acts, nor humiliating them at any occasion. By acting this manner, we will love our enemies.

For the spiritist, who thinks over and regards the past and the future, loving one's enemies is an act of wisdom. The spiritist thanks God for the trials and contacts with the opponents who offer them the opportunity to learn how to have patience and resignation. The truly superior individual is not offended by the insults from people yet inferior. The noble and generous soul is superior.

The discarnate enemies

The spiritist has extra reasons to learn to love one's enemies. One knows that death only frees us from the physical body and from an opponent's presence, but the opponent can keep on wishing us bad after death. A revenging action from us can only provoke irritation and greater reaction from our enemy, once life goes on. Revenge raises only more revenge and most of the time this is the punishment for those who couldn't forgive.

Therefore, there are incarnate and discarnate enemies. Discarnate enemies pursue us whenever we deserve it by obsessing and subjugating us, and this persecution end up helping us out in our process of evolvement. As there are malevolent people on earth, there are also malevolent spirits in the terrestrial circle. The best way to improve them is by exercising charity, which does not only inhibit the growth of the evil but also shows the path for the good.

Whoever shall smite you on your right cheek turn to him the other also

> You have heard that it was said, 'Eye for eye, and tooth for tooth.' But I tell you, Do not resist an evil person. If someone strikes you on the right cheek, turn to him the other also. And if someone wants to sue you and take your tunic, let him have your cloak as well. If someone forces you to go one mile, go with him two miles. Give to the one who asks you, and do not turn away from the one who wants to borrow from you. (Matthew, chapter 5: 38-42)

Back to the Moses' time, 'Eye for eye, and tooth for tooth' was considered a fair thought. And Christ's teaching may seem cowardice for a proud individual, because one can't figure out that there is more courage in bearing an offense than in breaking out a revenge (even though one's view does not go beyond the present moment).

Certainly Jesus' words cannot be literally considered because this would be the same as sentencing all the reactions to the evil, letting a free way for bad people's actions.

Jesus mentioned through his words that revenge was condemning, but he didn't try to avoid fair defense of the offended person.

That means it's better being offended than offending, better bearing injustice with patience than making one, better being fooled than fooling. The faith in future life, in the justice of God, that nothing goes unpunished, must provide people with the necessary forces to stand the adversities with patience and resignation.

In this chapter, the spirits teach:

1. That revenge is one of the humanity's most savage habits.

2. That we should cultivate the motto "without charity there is no salvation" and never practice revenge.

3. That we spiritists should try to love those that cause indifference, hate and contempt, this way we can approach God.

4. That we shouldn't dodge the traced path because of the presence of trials, temptations and the ups and downs of the terrestrial life.

5. That God's kingdom will only be set on earth when there is no more dislike, arguments or wars.

6. That spiritists, being intellectually and morally clear minded, should not reply the aggressions they suffer.

7. That the cause of arguments and wars will disappear when charity is common among people, obeying the maxim that points out that we must not wish others what we do not wish for ourselves.

In this chapter, Kardec teaches:

1. Nowadays the death of a man is an event that causes commotion and this didn't happen in the past.

2. That Spiritism certainly contributes for the evolution of the customs, by spreading the feeling of charity and fraternity among human beings.

CHAPTER 13

DO NOT LET YOUR LEFT HAND KNOW WHAT YOUR RIGHT HAND IS DOING

Do good without ostentation

"Be careful not to do your 'acts of righteousness' before men, to be seen by them. If you do, you will have no reward from your Father in heaven. "So when you give to the needy, do not announce it with trumpets, as the hypocrites do in the synagogues and on the streets, to be honored by men. I tell you the truth, they have received their reward in full. But when you give to the needy, do not let your left hand know what your right hand is doing, so that your giving may be in secret. Then your Father, who sees what is done in secret, will reward you. (Matthew, chapter 6: 1-4)

When he came down from the mountainside, large crowds followed him. A man with leprosy came and knelt before him and said, "Lord, if you are willing, you can make me clean." Jesus reached out his hand and touched the man. "I am willing," he said. "Be clean!" Immediately he was cured of his leprosy. Then Jesus said to him, "See that you don't tell anyone. But go, show yourself to the priest and offer the gift Moses commanded, as a testimony to them." (Matthew, chapter 8: 1-4)

The individual who is keen so that everyone knows, when one is doing good, only shows that the person gives more value to this life than the afterlife. This person also gives less value to God, because if one did good in hidden, one would have His recognition (which is, according to the good spirits, what really matters).

The modesty that we should bear when we do the good is well defined by the sentence "do not let your left hand know what your right hand is doing." The good practiced silently represents moral and material charity, because it does not require public thanks from the benefited person by keeping his or her dignity. True charity is subtle and does not humiliate the one who receives it.

Hidden misfortunes

Many charitable actions only happen when disasters of great proportions occur, which generally move the public. But there are thousands of personal calamities that pass on unnoticed, often because the victims suffer without complaining. They are hidden misfortunes, bored in a discreet way and do not have a public appeal, but it should also be attended.

The widow's mite

> *Jesus sat down opposite the place where the offerings were put and watched the crowd putting their money into the temple treasury. Many rich people threw in large amounts. But a poor widow came and put in two very small copper coins, worth only a fraction of a penny. Calling his disciples to him, Jesus said, "I tell you the truth, this poor widow has put more into the treasury than all the others. They all gave out of their wealth; but she, out of her poverty, put in everything—all she had to live on." (Mark, chapter 12: 41-44. Luke, chapter 21: 1-4)*

Many argue they cannot do all the good they wish because they haven't enough money or resources to do so. They say they wish to be rich to put their wealth on charity. These desires, however, aren't so disinterested. In fact, deep down, many people want to earn more to take personal advantage of this wealth prior to direct resources for charitable purposes. This is not, however, true charity, because true charity only exists when the individual thinks of others before thinking of oneself.

Each one must do charity with the resources one has and earns through one's own effort and work, even though it seems little. Not only with money can a person be charitable, but also with volunteer work, donating time, and reducing resting hours for the benefit of others.

To invite the poor and the lame - To give without thought of recompense

> *Then Jesus said to his host, "When you give a luncheon or dinner, do not invite your friends, your brothers or relatives, or your rich neighbors; if you do, they may invite you back and so you will be repaid. But when you give a banquet, invite the poor, the crippled, the lame, the blind, and you will be blessed. Although they cannot repay you, you will be repaid at the resurrection of the righteous." (Luke, chapter 14: 12-15)*

Jesus spoke figuratively and had to use strong images as example to raise great effect on the people of his time. Of course Jesus would be unreasonable to advise his disciples to leave friends and relatives outside a banquet and invite only beggars. In fact, the meaning of Jesus' message was to advise us to do the good for the joy of doing it, and not seeking retribution. That's why the recommendation was to invite the poor, since they could not indeed payback.

We know that many only invite to their parties those who they are interested in and can repay the favor. And sometimes, they forget even less fortunate relatives, which may be the subject of charity in a discreet and disinterested way.

In this chapter, the spirits teach:

1. That if everyone followed the maxims of "do to others as you would wish them do to us and to love one another", everyone in the world would be happy, there would be no

poverty and the poor would have food that is left on the table of the rich.

2. That we should not hurt any unfortunate because we could thus be dealing with a sibling, parent, or even a friend of other lives, which will bring much distress when we recognize that person in the spirit world.

3. That we should also do moral charity, which does not have any material cost to those who practice it, but it is the most difficult to be exercised. And that moral charity means supporting one another.

4. That there are several ways to practice charity, for example, by thoughts, words and actions. By praying for the needy, giving advice and acting for the benefit of the needy, charity is being exercised.

5. That we should seek peace of heart and contentment of spirit in the exercise of charity, a true remedy for the afflictions we feel.

6. That there is much good to be done that awaits us, and that may bring us great joy when we return to the spirit plane.

7. That we must love each other and give up selfishness, so as we also have great joys.

8. That we should not disregard the teachings of Jesus, and that our problems come from our refusal to follow these teachings.

9. That charity is the most important virtue.

10. That we should not mistake charity with giving alms. That giving alms is useful, however it can be humiliating for the one who gives and the one who receives.

11. That Spiritists should be charitable to those who do not think the same way, inviting them to their meetings without shocking them or without imposing beliefs, always in a friendly manner.

12. That compassion is the virtue that brings us most closely to the spirit world. It tames all selfishness and pride inside of us and inclines us towards charity and love of neighbor.

13. That we should always help the weak, although gratitude cannot be assured.

14. That God allows the ingratitude to exist as a response of a good deed as to experience our capacity to continue exercising the good.

15. That the ungrateful spirit will understand the error of one's behavior when one discarnates, and will wish to fix it, even if only in another life. Therefore, the person who did good will have contributed to the moral advancement of the ungrateful and to oneself, because even without any reward the person will have practiced good deeds.

16. That the charity practiced exclusively among people of the same opinion, the same belief, or the same party does not have the same value. That the spirit of sect, party or any kind of domination among human beings is what needs to be extinct, because the true Christian sees one's brothers and sisters in everyone, regardless of belief, opinion or whatever.

17. That since Jesus recommended we should love even our enemies, it would be really bad if we missed the opportunity of benefiting a person because he or she had different beliefs or thoughts from ours.

CHAPTER 14

HONOR YOUR MOTHER AND YOUR FATHER

You know the commandments: 'Do not murder, do not commit adultery, do not steal, do not give false testimony, do not defraud, honor your father and mother.' (Mark, chapter 10: 19; Luke, chapter 17: 20; Matthew, chapter 19: 18-19)

"Honor your father and your mother, so that you may live long in the land the LORD your God is giving you. (Exodus, chapter 20: 12)

Filial devotion

This commandment is a consequence of the general law of charity and love for one's neighbor. The term honor includes an added duty in this regard: filial devotion. God wanted to show that to love, one must add respect, consideration, attention, obedience, which implies to fulfill toward our parents (or those who play this role) in an even stricter manner all that charity requires us to do for our neighbors. We must assist our parents in their needs, provide for their rest in old age, and surround them with the care they took of us in our childhood.

Those that do not have such gratitude to their parents will also suffer ingratitude and abandonment in this life or in a future one. Even when we have careless parents, it is for God to punish them and not their children. If charity establishes as a law that we should always pay evil with good and tolerate others' fault, how much more these obligations apply regarding one's parents? Any misconduct toward our neighbors is even worse when it is addressed to our parents, because in this case, besides being a lack of charity, it is also lack of gratitude.

Who is my mother and who are my brothers?

Then Jesus entered a house, and again a crowd gathered, so that he and his disciples were not even able to eat. When his family heard about this, they went to take charge of him, for they said, "He is out of his mind." Then Jesus' mother and brothers arrived. Standing outside, they sent someone in to call him. A crowd was sitting around him, and they told him, "Your mother and brothers are outside looking for you." "Who are my mother and my brothers?" he asked. Then he looked at those seated in a circle around him and said, "Here are my mother and my brothers! Whoever does God's will is my brother and sister and mother." (Mark, chapter 3: 20, 21 and 31-35. Matthew, chapter 12: 46-50)

Corporeal relationship and spiritual relationship

Blood ties do not necessarily establish ties among spirits. Of course, Jesus would never deny his mother or his brothers; what he wanted to explain to us in this passage of the Gospel is that the body proceeds from the body but the spirit does not proceed from the spirit, because the spirit already existed before the formation of the body. That is, parents do not create the spirit of their children; they simply generate their bodies. However, they have the obligation to aid their children in the development of their intelligence and character in order to help them progress.

Spirits who incarnate in the same family (especially among close relatives) are in most cases, spirits connected by ties of affection that come from previous incarnations. But they could also be complete strangers, or even people who hated one another in previous lives, and now they incarnate in the same family as a trial. True family ties are not blood ties, but ties of sympathy and similarity of ideas that connect spirits *before*, *during* and *after* their incarnations. This explains why two individuals born from different parents can understand and enjoy each other better than two blood brothers.

Consequently there are two types of families: families through corporeal ties (terrestrial family) and families through spirit ties. The first are fragile and can end over time; the latter are permanent and continue beyond the corporeal life. And this is what Jesus meant when he said. "Here are my mother and my brothers." He wanted to show that the spiritual family is the one that really counts, since it remains after death and is based on sympathy and attraction between the spirits.

In this chapter, the spirits teach:

1. That the ingratitude comes from selfishness and it is always bad, but the ingratitude of children to parents is even worse and more reprehensible.

2. That the password to reach God is only one: charity. And there is no love without forgiveness.

3. That many spirits are asked to incarnate among those who hurt them in other incarnations to undergo a trial in order to progress.

4. That either failing or overcoming this trial will depend on these spirits. They may choose to become friends or to continue being enemies.

5. That spiritists must understand that the souls of their children come from space to make progress and it is their duty to bring them up toward goodness and get them closer to God.

6. That parents should strive to accept and understand even the child who gives them grief, because that child can be an enemy of the past who is there to make amends.

7. That it is the duty of parents to teach children that they are on earth to improve, and guide them to love others and to do good.

8. That parents should fight so as pride and selfishness do not develop in their children, otherwise they may reap ingratitude. Parents who have done everything they could and

yet could not improve their children's character will not be held responsible. They may rest assured that this change will come one day.

9. God does not provide a trial heavier than the person is able to withstand. That is, if they fail those tests, it is simply due to lack of will rather than lack of capacity.

10. That God always allows regret, and we should thank Him for trials that help us to move forward.

11. That the toughest tests are those that affect the heart, but there is no eternal despair and God will not let anyone suffer forever.

12. That it depends on us ending up with our own suffering, through the effort of evolution. To do that, we must see beyond the present incarnation and have patience, trusting that everything will be fine.

13. That if we look beyond this incarnation, we may understand the real ties that bind the spirits, and see that those ties become stronger with reincarnation, rather than breaking.

14. That the moral similarities among spirits are the true bridge between them. The spirits united by affection always seek one another to come together, forming spiritual families that oftentimes incarnate together.

15. That even when these friendly spirits are separated in some incarnation, they always meet later again.

16. That less developed spirits may incarnate within these "spiritual families" to receive advice and good examples. The disturbances they often cause may serve as trials for the most advanced spirits of these "families".

CHAPTER 15

WITHOUT CHARITY THERE IS NO SALVATION

What the spirit need in order to be saved – Parable of the Good Samaritan

"When the Son of Man comes in his glory, and all the angels with him, he will sit on his throne in heavenly glory. All the nations will be gathered before him, and he will separate the people one from another as a shepherd separates the sheep from the goats. He will put the sheep on his right and the goats on his left "Then the King will say to those on his right, 'Come, you who are blessed by my Father; take your inheritance, the kingdom prepared for you since the creation of the world. For I was hungry and you gave me something to eat, I was thirsty and you gave me something to drink, I was a stranger and you invited me in, I needed clothes and you clothed me, I was sick and you looked after me, I was in prison and you came to visit me.' "Then the righteous will answer him, 'Lord, when did we see you hungry and feed you, or thirsty and give you something to drink? When did we see you a stranger and invite you in, or needing clothes and clothe you? When did we see you sick or in prison and go to visit you?' "The King will reply, 'I tell you the truth, whatever you did for one of the least of these brothers of mine, you did for me.' "Then he will say to those on his left, 'Depart from me, you who are cursed, into the eternal fire prepared for the devil and his angels. For I was hungry and you gave me nothing to eat, I was thirsty and you gave me nothing to drink, I was a stranger and you did not invite me in, I needed clothes and you did not clothe me, I was sick and in prison and you did not look after me.' "They also will answer, 'Lord, when did we see you hungry or thirsty or a stranger or needing clothes or sick or in prison, and did not help you?' "He will reply, 'I tell you the truth, whatever you did not do for one of the least of these, you did not do for me.' "Then they will go away to eternal punishment, but the righteous to eternal life." (Matthew, chapter 25: 31-46)

On one occasion an expert in the law stood up to test Jesus. "Teacher," he asked, "what must I do to inherit eternal life?" "What is written in the Law?" he replied. "How do you read it?" He answered: " 'Love the Lord your God with all your heart and with all your soul and with all your strength and with all your mind'; and, 'Love your neighbor as yourself.' "You have answered correctly," Jesus replied. "Do this and you will live." But he wanted to justify himself, so he asked Jesus, "And who is my neighbor?" In reply Jesus said: "A man was going down from Jerusalem to Jericho, when he fell into the hands of robbers. They stripped him of his clothes, beat him and went away, leaving him half dead. A priest happened to be going down the same road, and when he saw the man, he passed by on the other side. So too, a Levite, when he came to the place and saw him, passed by on the other side. But a Samaritan, as he traveled, came where the man was; and when he saw him, he took pity on him. He went to him and bandaged his wounds, pouring on oil and wine. Then he put the man on his own donkey, took him to an inn and took care of him. The next day he took out two silver coins and gave them to the innkeeper. 'Look after him,' he said, 'and when I return, I will reimburse you for any extra expense you may have.'

"Which of these three do you think was a neighbor to the man who fell into the hands of robbers?" The expert in the law replied, "The one who had mercy on him." Jesus told him, "Go and do likewise."(Luke, chapter 10: 25-37)

All of Jesus' morals are summed up in charity and humility (which is the opposite of selfishness and pride), and he points these two virtues as being the way to eternal happiness. Just remember what He said: that the kingdom of heaven belongs to the humble ones; and that the peacemakers, the merciful and the pure of heart are blessed. He said that we should love our neighbor, our enemies as ourselves, and we should forgive offenses and do toward others as we would have them do toward us, that we should do good without ostentation and judge ourselves before judging others.

In the passage from Matthew, we can clearly understand that happiness is reserved for the good ones, while the wicked is bound to be unhappy. In order to separate them (the good from the wicked) Jesus highlights only one thing: the practice of charity. He is not interested in what faith one professes, and does not segregate anyone by religion: the only thing that differs one from the other is charity, which is considered the only condition for salvation. Jesus places charity on the first plane of virtues, because charity implicitly entails all the others: humility, kindness, benevolence, justice and forgiveness, among others, and because it is the complete negation of pride and selfishness.

The greatest of the commandments

Hearing that Jesus had silenced the Sadducees, the Pharisees got together. One of them, an expert in the law, tested him with this question: "Teacher, which is the greatest commandment in the Law?" Jesus replied: " 'Love the Lord your God with all your heart and with all your soul and with all your mind.' This is the first and greatest commandment. And the second is like it: 'Love your neighbor as yourself.' All the Law and the Prophets hang on these two commandments." (Matthew, chapter 22: 34-40)

Jesus made it clear that one cannot truly love God without loving one's neighbor, nor can one love one's neighbor without loving God. Thus, everything that is done against one's neighbor is also done against God. In fact, it's all summed up in the sentence: *Without charity there is no salvation.*

The need for charity according to Paul

If I speak in the tongues of men and of angels, but have not love, I am only a resounding gong or a clanging cymbal. If I have the gift of prophecy and can fathom all mysteries and all knowledge, and if I have a faith that can move mountains, but have not love, I am nothing. If I give all I

101

possess to the poor and surrender my body to the flames, but have not love, I gain nothing. Love is patient, love is kind. It does not envy, it does not boast, it is not proud. It is not rude, it is not self-seeking, it is not easily angered, it keeps no record of wrongs. Love does not delight in evil but rejoices with the truth. It always protects, always trusts, always hopes, always perseveres. And now these three remain: faith, hope and love. But the greatest of these is love. (Paul, 1 Corinthians, chapter 13: 1-7, 13)

The apostle Paul, through this Gospel passage, explains that charity is within everyone's reach: the ignorant and the learned, the rich and the poor, because it is independent of any particular belief system. He shows that true charity is not only displayed in beneficence, but in the gathering of all qualities of heart, in goodness and benevolence toward others.

Without the church there is no salvation. Without the truth there is no salvation.

While the maxim "without charity there is no salvation" is based on a universal principal and gives all God's children access to happiness," the one "without the Church there is no salvation" excludes many people (those who are not of this "church"), denying them the possibility of future happiness. This phrase also divides the children of God, rather than unite them, and take people apart from each other, raising among them anger, discord and prejudice. The maxim "without charity there is no salvation" consecrates the principle of equality before God and freedom of conscience; in addition, assuring that "without the Church there is no salvation" is totally contrary to Jesus' teachings. Saying that "without the truth there is no salvation" is the same as saying that "without the Church there is no salvation," since all religions believe they have the real truth. The absolute truth is shared only among spirits of the highest order. Humans can aspire only to relative truth proportional to their advancement.

Spiritism believes that one can be saved whatever one's belief may be, provided that one observes God's laws.

In this chapter, the spirits teach:

1. That those who practice charity will live in peace on earth and be in a good place in the spirit realm.

2. That nothing expresses more accurately the thought of Jesus and nothing sums up so perfectly the duties of people as the maxim "without charity there is no salvation."

3. That if the individual is guided by the practice of charity one would never go astray.

4. That charity prevents the practice of evil and makes people practice good deeds.

5. That we should thank God for the privilege of knowing Spiritism, not because it provides us with salvation more than other religions, but because it helps us understand the teachings of Jesus and makes us better people.

6. That we, spiritists, must strive to set a good example, showing those around us that the true Spiritists and the true Christians are one and the same, since all those who practice charity are legitimate followers of Jesus, no matter what religion they profess.

IT IS NOT POSSIBLE TO SERVE BOTH GOD AND MAMMON

The salvation of the rich

"No servant can serve two masters. Either he will hate the one and love the other, or he will be devoted to the one and despise the other. You cannot serve both God and Money." (Luke, chapter 16: 13)

A certain ruler asked him, "Good teacher, what must I do to inherit eternal life?" "Why do you call me good?" Jesus answered. "No one is good—except God alone. You know the commandments: 'Do not commit adultery, do not murder, do not steal, do not give false testimony, honor your father and mother.'" "All these I have kept since I was a boy," he said. When Jesus heard this, he said to him, "You still lack one thing. Sell everything you have and give to the poor, and you will have treasure in heaven. Then come, follow me." When he heard this, he became very sad, because he was a man of great wealth. Jesus looked at him and said, "How hard it is for the rich to enter the kingdom of God! Indeed, it is easier for a camel to go through the eye of a needle than for a rich man to enter the kingdom of God." (Luke, chapter 18: 18-25; Mark, chapter 10: 17-25)

Guard yourself from avarice

Someone in the crowd said to him, "Teacher, tell my brother to divide the inheritance with me." Jesus replied, "Man, who appointed me a judge or an arbiter between you?" Then he said to them, "Watch out! Be on your guard against all kinds of greed; a man's life does not consist in the abundance of his possessions." And he told them this parable: "The ground of a certain rich man produced a good crop. He thought to himself, 'What shall I do? I have no place to store my crops.' "Then he said, 'This is what I'll do. I will tear down my barns and build bigger ones, and there I will store all my grain and my goods. And I'll say to myself, "You have plenty of good things laid up for many years. Take life easy; eat, drink and be merry." "But God said to him, 'You fool! This very night your life will be demanded from you. Then who will get what you have prepared for yourself?' "This is how it will be with anyone who stores up things for himself but is not rich toward God." (Luke, chapter 12: 13-21)

Jesus at Zacchaeus' house

Jesus entered Jericho and was passing through. A man was there by the name of Zacchaeus; he was a chief tax collector and was wealthy. He wanted to see who Jesus was, but being a short man he could not, because of the crowd. So he ran ahead and climbed a sycamore-fig tree to see him, since Jesus was coming that way. When Jesus reached the spot, he looked up and said to him, "Zacchaeus, come down immediately. I must stay at your house today." So he came down at once and welcomed him gladly.

All the people saw this and began to mutter, "He has gone to be the guest of a 'sinner.'" But Zacchaeus stood up and said to the Lord, "Look, Lord! Here and now I give half of my possessions to the poor, and if I have cheated anybody out of anything, I will pay back four times the amount."

Jesus said to him, "Today salvation has come to this house, because this man, too, is a son of Abraham. For the Son of Man came to seek and to save what was lost." (Luke, chapter 19: 1-10)

Parable of the bad rich man

"There was a rich man who was dressed in purple and fine linen and lived in luxury every day. At his gate was laid a beggar named Lazarus, covered with sores and longing to eat what fell from the rich man's table. Even the dogs came and licked his sores. "The time came when the beggar died and the angels carried him to Abraham's side. The rich man also died and was buried. In hell, where he was in torment, he looked up and saw Abraham far away, with Lazarus by his side. So he called to him, 'Father Abraham, have pity on

me and send Lazarus to dip the tip of his finger in water and cool my tongue, because I am in agony in this fire.' "But Abraham replied, 'Son, remember that in your lifetime you received your good things, while Lazarus received bad things, but now he is comforted here and you are in agony. And besides all this, between us and you a great chasm has been fixed, so that those who want to go from here to you cannot, nor can anyone cross over from there to us.' "He answered, 'Then I beg you, father, send Lazarus to my father's house, for I have five brothers. Let him warn them, so that they will not also come to this place of torment.' "Abraham replied, 'They have Moses and the Prophets; let them listen to them.'" 'No, father Abraham,' he said, 'but if someone from the dead goes to them, they will repent.' "He said to him, 'If they do not listen to Moses and the Prophets, they will not be convinced even if someone rises from the dead.' " (Luke, chapter 16: 19-31)*

Parable of the talents[1]

"Again, it will be like a man going on a journey, who called his servants and entrusted his property to them. To one he gave five talents of money, to another two talents, and to another one talent, each according to his ability. Then he went on his journey. The man who had received the five talents went at once and put his money to work and gained five more. So also, the one with the two talents gained two more. But the man who had received the one talent went off, dug a hole in the ground and hid his master's money. "After a long time the master of those servants returned and settled accounts with them. The man who had received the five talents brought the other five. 'Master,' he said, 'you entrusted me with five talents. See, I have gained five more.' "His master replied, 'Well done, good and faithful servant! You have been faithful with a few things; I will put you in charge of many things. Come and share your master's happiness!' "The man with the two talents also came. 'Master,' he said, 'you entrusted me with two talents; see, I have gained two more.' "His master replied, 'Well done,

---

[1] Talent was a coin used in Ancient Greece and Rome.

good and faithful servant! You have been faithful with a few things; I will put you in charge of many things. Come and share your master's happiness!' "Then the man who had received the one talent came. 'Master,' he said, 'I knew that you are a hard man, harvesting where you have not sown and gathering where you have not scattered seed. So I was afraid and went out and hid your talent in the ground. See, here is what belongs to you.' "His master replied, 'You wicked, lazy servant! So you knew that I harvest where I have not sown and gather where I have not scattered seed? Well then, you should have put my money on deposit with the bankers, so that when I returned I would have received it back with interest. " 'Take the talent from him and give it to the one who has the ten talents. For everyone who has will be given more, and he will have abundance. Whoever does not have, even what he has will be taken from him. And throw that worthless servant outside, into the darkness, where there will be weeping and gnashing of teeth.' (Matthew, chapter 25: 14-30)

The providential usefulness of riches – Trials of riches and poverty

If wealth were an impediment to the salvation of people (as it seems to be the case if we follow literally certain words from Jesus) God wouldn't have put it in the hands of some. But wealth is in fact a very slippery trial, more dangerous than poverty because of its allure, the temptation it creates and the fascination it exerts; it fosters selfishness and pride, and it's the strongest tie that keeps human bound to earth.

However, even though wealth makes the journey difficult, it doesn't mean that it cannot became a means of salvation. All depends in how wealth is utilized.

When Jesus proposed to the young man to sell everything he owned and to follow him, he only wanted to show that being too concerned with material assets is an obstacle to salvation. He wanted to show that it's not good enough to follow only certain commandments; it's not good

108

enough not to engage in wrongdoing; however it is a must to be good. In other words, it is needed to practice charity.

Jesus did not ask the elimination of wealth, and much less condemned the honest work that could procure it, because that would be against the law of progress, which is God's law.

If riches are the source of many ills, that's people's fault, who misuse it, just as they misuse many other gifts. If wealth could produce only bad things God wouldn't have put it on earth. It is up to humans to know how to use it and to make it produce the good. It is people's mission to work for the material improvement of the planet, increasing production with the help of Science, Economics, and the good relations and communications among all people. It was necessity that made the human beings to create wealth and to reveal Science, which helps them in the development of their own intelligence, and will help them later on to understand the great moral truths. The possibility of obtaining wealth on earth motivates people to study, to work and to put effort, and that's the reason it is considered an element of progress.

The inequality of riches

If only the current life is considered, the inequality of riches is a difficult problem to be solved. Why aren't all equally rich? Due to a simple reason: because not all are equally intelligent or arduous workers to obtain wealth, nor equally serious and wise to conserve it. If wealth were divided equally, it would give each person a minimal and insufficient portion; that if such division were carried out, the equilibrium would soon be shattered due to the diversity in character and aptitudes; if everyone found themselves with a guaranteed sustenance, they wouldn't put effort and hard work into anything. Moreover, without the possibility of obtaining wealth, people wouldn't have the necessary motivation to create and work for the great discoveries and endeavors that bring us the common wealth.

But why does God grant wealth to people who don't put it into something good? Because it is up to people to decide which path to take; that's why people have freewill. Practicing good actions aren't impositions from God, but are the results of our own efforts and determination. Wealth is a way of God testing the human beings morally, besides being also a powerful means of inducing progress. God does not wish for it to remain unproductive for long and thus moves it around incessantly. Hence, each individual possesses it in turn. The one who doesn't possess it today has either had it already or will have it in a future life; and the one who possess it now might not have it tomorrow. Being rich may be a trial of charity and abnegation while being poor may be a trial of patience and resignation. This way, when we consider the set of corporeal existences, we observe that everything balances out justly. The source of the evil resides in selfishness and pride. Abuses of every kind will cease by themselves when humankind rules itself according to the law of charity.

In this chapter, spirits teach us:

1. That an individual truly owns only what it takes with him or her after discarnating and that no one can take away from a person: intelligence, knowledge, and moral qualities.

2. That these virtues are the actual riches that we really have to worry about accumulating.

3. That a good spiritual condition cannot be bought in any way; that it must be conquered through practicing good actions.

4. That the goods of earth belong to God, who grants them to be handled in the best way possible.

5. That legitimate riches are those obtained through effort and honest work, without causing harm to others.

6. That people must not overuse riches and possessions, nor misuse them by satisfying their own self-importance and pride as this would nullify the merit of their effort and work.

7. That the commandment "Love one another" and the practice of charity must always drive us in how to apply our riches.

8. That the concern with perfecting our moral behavior must be infinitely more important than concerning with our material well being.

9. That all people are only administrators of the assets that God has put in their hands, and they will be held responsible for the use of those assets.

10. That the good use of wealth means using it for the good of others, and that misuse it means applying it only to our own satisfaction.

11. That the riches may and must be applied for the general well being, and that giving alms is not the best way to accomplish this.

12. That loving physical wealth is one of the greatest obstacles to moral and spiritual advancement.

13. That the rich must give without ostentation and the poor must receive humbly.

14. That throwing away and wasting wealth does not demonstrate one is unattached and uncommitted to it, but it shows unconcern and indifference.

15. That being unattached to wealth means use it for the benefit of others, and not only for self-benefit, besides accepting its eventual loss.

16. That we must know how to live without wealth when we don't have it, employ it wisely when we have it, and know how to give it up when needed.

17. That we must learn how to be happy with very little.

18. That all have legitimate rights of leaving their assets to the inheritors, as God can always take that away, if necessary.

CHAPTER 17

BE PERFECT

The characteristics of perfection

But I tell you: Love your enemies and pray for those who persecute you. If you love those who love you, what reward will you get? Are not even the tax collectors doing that? And if you greet only your brothers, what are you doing more than others? Do not even pagans do that? Be perfect, therefore, as your heavenly Father is perfect. (Matthew, chapter 5: 44 & 46-48)

This passage, if taken literally, would make it seem that it is possible for us to achieve absolute perfection. But the creature cannot be as perfect as the Creator, because otherwise it would be like Him, which is impossible.

We can surely achieve a relative perfection, as Matthew's text wants to express. We can achieve this relative perfection if we do what Jesus taught us: to love our enemies, to do good to those who do not like us, and to pray for those who persecute us. In this way Jesus shows that the essence of perfection is charity. Love towards others (even enemies) is what brings us as close as possible to the perfection of the heavenly Father

The good persons

Good persons are those who practice the law of justice, love and charity, and always ask themselves if they have done unto others everything they would like others have done unto themselves. They have faith in God and in the future; thus, they place spiritual possessions above material ones. They accept the pains of life without complaint, because they know that atonement or trials are necessary for their development. They have great joy in doing good and comforting those that suffer, and are always thinking of others before thinking of themselves. Good persons are kind, humane, and benevolent towards all regardless of race or creed, because they regard all people as their brothers and sisters.

In all circumstances charity is their guide. They hold no hatred or rancor, or desire for vengeance, and always forgive and forget offenses. They are indulgent toward others' weaknesses, and they study their imperfections and strive incessantly to combat them.

They do not gloat over their wealth or their personal advantages, for they know that everything that has been given to them can be taken away.

They use but do not abuse the possessions that have been accorded to them, for they are a trust for which they have to render an accounting. Good persons respect their fellow beings and their rights.

The good spiritist

If properly understood and practiced, Spiritism leads everyone to goodness. Nevertheless, there are many Spiritists that do not apply these teachings in their lives. Why? Spiritism is clear and transparent in the lessons it teaches, it does not require great intelligence to be understood, but it is necessary to have the *maturity of the moral sense*. And that maturity does not depend on age or education level, it depends only on the spiritual development of the incarnate spirit.

Some Spiritists still care only about the phenomenon, and forget the most important aspect of Spiritism: the moral. While some are content with their limited horizons, others understand that there is something better, they make the effort to free themselves and they always reach their goal if they maintain a firm will. *True Spiritists are recognized by their moral transformation and the efforts they make to overcome their evil inclinations.*

114

Parable of the sower

That same day Jesus went out of the house and sat by the lake. Such large crowds gathered around him that he got into a boat and sat in it, while all the people stood on the shore. Then he told them many things in parables, saying: "A farmer went out to sow his seed. As he was scattering the seed, some fell along the path, and the birds came and ate it up. Some fell on rocky places, where it did not have much soil. It sprang up quickly, because the soil was shallow. But when the sun came up, the plants were scorched, and they withered because they had no root. Other seed fell among thorns, which grew up and choked the plants. Still other seed fell on good soil, where it produced a crop—a hundred, sixty or thirty times what was sown. He who has ears, let him hear." (Matthew, chapter 13: 1-9)

"Listen then to what the parable of the sower means: When anyone hears the message about the kingdom and does not understand it, the evil one comes and snatches away what was sown in his heart. This is the seed sown along the path. The one who received the seed that fell on rocky places is the man who hears the word and at once receives it with joy. But since he has no root, he lasts only a short time. When trouble or persecution comes because of the word, he quickly falls away. The one who received the seed that fell among the thorns is the man who hears the word, but the worries of this life and the deceitfulness of wealth choke it, making it unfruitful. But the one who received the seed that fell on good soil is the man who hears the word and understands it. He produces a crop, yielding a hundred, sixty or thirty times what was sown." (Matthew, chapter 13: 18-23)

The parable of the sower represents perfectly the nuances that exist in the ways one profits from the teachings of the Gospel. For many, these lessons do not help, like the seed that has fallen on the stony soil, produces no crop.

And that also happens among the Spiritists. There are some who are interest only in the physical phenomena but derive nothing of consequence from them There are others who seek nothing but the wonder in spirit communications, but do not become any better after that. There are still others who find the counsels to be very good for others, but do not apply them in their own lives. However, there are certainly many of them who learn a lot with these teachings, just as the seed that falls on good soil and yields a crop.

In this chapter, the spirits teach:

1. That the moral duty of each one of us starts at the point when our neighbor's happiness or tranquility is threatened.

2. That we are all equal in relation to pain, no matter we are small or big, ignorant or educated.

3. That God wants all his children not to do evil. For that reason everyone is taught by life experiences.

3. That the individual, who does one's duty, loves God more than people and loves people more than oneself.

4. That true virtue does not promote itself, that the virtuous individual simply does good with disinterest and self-disregard, without expecting any recognition, praise or reward.

5. That little virtue with modesty is worthier than a lot of virtue with pride.

6. That authority, or the power of command that a person is given by God is a mission or a trial, and can be withdrawn by Him at any time.

7. The person that holds this power will account for how one will use it. The person will be responsible for guidelines and examples one gives to one's subordinates, both for evil and for good.

8. If that person follows the teachings of Christ, one will treat their subordinates fairly and equally, never despising

them or considering them inferior, once one knows that the social differences are not important in the eyes of God.

9. The one who commands nowadays or in other lives (past or future) may be in a position to serve, and vice versa.

10. That an employee also has duties to perform; even when one's boss does not meet its own, since no one has the right to repay evil with evil.

11. That an employee, even when in a position of stress, should behave with one's boss the way one would like to behave with him or her if one was the boss.

12. That no one should get isolated from the world, but live among others, since perfection is the practice of absolute love, and this is only possible when we live in society.

13. That people should strive to be happy, but always in good conscience toward God and others.

14. It is necessary to take care of our bodies and our health, since the body is an instrument of the soul, and it is also through it that the soul becomes perfect.

15. That perfection is not attained through the sacrifice of the body, but rather in the transformation of the spirit.

CHAPTER 18

MANY ARE CALLED BUT FEW ARE CHOSEN

Parable of the wedding feast

Jesus spoke to them again in parables, saying: "The kingdom of heaven is like a king who prepared a wedding banquet for his son. He sent his servants to those who had been invited to the banquet to tell them to come, but they refused to come. "Then he sent some more servants and said, 'Tell those who have been invited that I have prepared my dinner: My oxen and fattened cattle have been butchered, and everything is ready. Come to the wedding banquet.' "But they paid no attention and went off—one to his field, another to his business. The rest seized his servants, mistreated them and killed them. The king was enraged. He sent his army and destroyed those murderers and burned their city.

"Then he said to his servants, 'The wedding banquet is ready, but those I invited did not deserve to come. Go to the street corners and invite to the banquet anyone you find.' So the servants went out into the streets and gathered all the people they could find, both good and bad, and the wedding hall was filled with guests. "But when the king came in to see the guests, he noticed a man there who was not wearing wedding clothes. 'Friend,' he asked, 'how did you get in here without wedding clothes?' The man was speechless. "Then the king told the attendants, 'Tie him hand and foot, and throw him outside, into the darkness, where there will be weeping and gnashing of teeth.' "For many are invited, but few are chosen." (Matthew, chapter 22: 1-14)

In this parable, Jesus compares the kingdom of heaven to a wedding party. Speaking of the ones whom had first been invited, he referred to the Jews, who were the first to know of Jesus' teaching, but who ended up rejecting them and allowing him to be crucified. Those sent by the king (his servants) symbolize the prophets, whose mission it was to teach the road of true happiness, but they were barely heard and, in some cases, even massacred. Those who had been invited but did not come, claiming they had private business matters to take care of, are the worldly ones, who are so busy with earthly things they have no time or inclination to learn of heavenly matters. When Jesus says that the king told his servants to invite anyone at all to come to the feast, whether they were bad or good, he meant that the word of God would then be taken to all peoples.

But the parable also teaches us that it is not enough to be invited or even to take a seat at the table to partake of the celestial banquet; it is also necessary to "be dressed in a nuptial tunic", in other words, have a pure heart and obey the law, which can be summarized in the aphorism "Without charity there is no salvation." Since there are few who hear God's words and actually follow them, we can say that many are those who are called to the kingdom of God but few are those chosen to enter it.

The narrow door

"Enter through the narrow gate. For wide is the gate and broad is the road that leads to destruction, and many enter through it. But small is the gate and narrow the road that leads to life, and only a few find it. (Matthew, chapter 7: 13, 14)

Someone asked him, "Lord, are only a few people going to be saved?" He said to them, "Make every effort to enter through the narrow door, because many, I tell you, will try to enter and will not be able to. Once the owner of the house gets up and closes the door, you will stand outside knocking and pleading, 'Sir, open the door for us.' "But he will answer, 'I don't know you or where you come from.' "Then you will say, 'We ate and drank with you, and you taught in our streets.' "But he will reply, 'I don't know you or where you come from. Away from me, all you evildoers!' "There will be weeping there, and gnashing of teeth, when you see

Abraham, Isaac and Jacob and all the prophets in the
kingdom of God, but you yourselves thrown out. People will
come from east and west and north and south, and will take
their places at the feast in the kingdom of God. Indeed there
are those who are last who will be first, and first who will
be last." (Luke, chapter 13: 23-30)

The path that leads to evil (or the road to perdition as Matthew called it) is wide, because it serves the majority of all men and women. On the other hand the door or path that leads to salvation is narrow, because only those who make enormous efforts to dominate their lower tendencies - something few of us are willing to do - get a chance to go through it. That is why "many are called but few are chosen."

And this happens on earth because for the moment (it is a temporary situation) evil still predominates here. When that part of humanity, which incarnates on earth, has evolved enough, there will be more people on the path to benevolence.

And why do we have so many hardships and problems? Why is the door so narrow? Why are so few able to get through it? The only way to come to terms with this is by taking reincarnation into account. We'll never be able to deeply understand Christ's teaching unless we understand that we have lived other lives and will live many more; that the past, present and future are always connected; that all of us will one day be able to go through that narrow door. After all, if we had just one life, where would God's justice be? Why would he allow the door to be so narrow that only a privileged few could get through it?

Not all those who say: Lord! Lord! Will enter into the kingdom of heaven

"Not everyone who says to me, 'Lord, Lord,' will enter the
kingdom of heaven, but only he who does the will of my
Father who is in heaven. Many will say to me on that day,
'Lord, Lord, did we not prophesy in your name, and in your

name drive out demons and perform many miracles?' Then I will tell them plainly, 'I never knew you. Away from me, you evildoers!' (Matthew, chapter 7: 21-23)

"Therefore everyone who hears these words of mine and puts them into practice is like a wise man who built his house on the rock. The rain came down, the streams rose, and the winds blew and beat against that house; yet it did not fall, because it had its foundation on the rock. But everyone who hears these words of mine and does not put them into practice is like a foolish man who built his house on sand. The rain came down, the streams rose, and the winds blew and beat against that house, and it fell with a great crash." (Matthew, chapter 7: 24-27; Luke, chapter 6: 46-49)

Anyone who breaks one of the least of these commandments and teaches others to do the same will be called least in the kingdom of heaven, but whoever practices and teaches these commands will be called great in the kingdom of heaven. (Matthew, chapter 5: 19)

It's pointless to make a show of love for Jesus with words if we don't make his words live and breathe in our daily actions. External acts of devotion (like rituals, hymns, ceremonies, etc) are meaningless unless they are accompanied by a steadfast abstinence from the practice of evil. To spend a whole day in prayer and not follow it with charity toward one's neighbors is to waste a whole day. Indeed, Jesus condemned those whose actions (or lack thereof) turned their words into lies.

Much will be asked of the one who receives much

That servant who knows his master's will and does not get ready or does not do what his master wants will be beaten with many blows. But the one who does not know and does things deserving punishment will be beaten with few blows. From everyone who has been given much, much will be demanded; and from the one who has been entrusted with much, much more will be asked. (Luke, chapter 12: 47, 48) Jesus said, "For judgment I have come into this world, so that the blind will see and those who see will become blind." Some Pharisees who were with him heard him say this and asked, "What? Are we blind too?" Jesus said, "If you were blind, you would not be guilty of sin; but now that you claim you can see, your guilt remains. (John, chapter 9: 39-41)

Whoever knows Christ's teachings and doesn't practice them is certainly guilty. But all does not know the Gospel, since only Christian groups use it as their guide. And, even among the followers of these groups, there are many who don't read the Gospel, and many others who do not understand it.

It is precisely for that reason that the spirits' teachings are so important. They place the Gospel within reach of all people, whether they are learned or ignorant, faithful or incredulous, Christian or non-Christian. And that happens because the spirits communicate everywhere. Thus whoever knows these teachings and doesn't practice them is even guiltier, since the truth is within their reach.

In the case of the mediums who transmit words from the good spirits, this problem becomes even more serious. They should learn the lessons they transmit before others and practice these lessons in their own behavior.

When Jesus says that "if you were blind, you would not sin", he meant that the greater someone's knowledge of divine law, the greater their guilt. To put it another way, the greater their ability to understand, to see, God's teachings, the more responsible they are for their actions, right or wrong. All else being equal, therefore, the ignorant are less guilty than the learned.

This being the case, much will be asked from us as Spiritists, since the privilege of knowing the truth was given to us. Spiritism comes to multiply the number of those who are called (those in touch with Christ's teachings) and, by showing the path of benevolence, it will also multiply the number of those who are chosen (those who apply these teachings in their lives.)

In this chapter, the spirits teach:

1. That we should preserve and cultivate Jesus' teachings

2. That once the seed of benevolence is planted in our hearts and cultivated by our own efforts, it can only bear good fruit.

3. That it's not enough to say "I'm a Christian" to be one of Christ's real followers, one must actually put his teachings into practice.

4. That the real Christian is not recognized by words, but by one's deeds.

CHAPTER 19

FAITH TRANSPORTS MOUNTAIN

When they came to the crowd, a man approached Jesus and knelt before him. "Lord, have mercy on my son," he said. "He has seizures and is suffering greatly. He often falls into the fire or into the water. I brought him to your disciples, but they could not heal him." "O unbelieving and perverse generation," Jesus replied, "how long shall I stay with you? How long shall I put up with you? Bring the boy here to me." Jesus rebuked the demon, and it came out of the boy, and he was healed from that moment. Then the disciples came to Jesus in private and asked, "Why couldn't we drive it out?" He replied, "Because you have so little faith. I tell you the truth, if you have faith as small as a mustard seed, you can say to this mountain, 'Move from here to there' and it will move. Nothing will be impossible for you." (Matthew, chapter 17: 14-20)

The mountain faith can move represents the array of problems people working to enhance the spiritual growth of humanity have to address, like ill will, prejudices, greed, selfishness, pride and fanaticisms among others. Only real faith provides the perseverance, resources and energy we need to remove the obstacles before us, both large and small.

Faith is also the confidence that we are capable of getting things done, the certainty that we can reach an objective. Those who have faith and act with conviction can handle the most difficult tasks without hesitation. And real faith is always calm and patient, since it is based on a clear understanding of reality.

But we mustn't confuse faith with arrogance. Faith is humble and comes from having more confidence in God than in oneself, since nothing can be accomplished without His help.

The phenomena of spiritual healing are only possible because of the faith that comes to place during magnetic action.

Those who have both great faith and great fluidic power can heal simply by willing it; this is part of the natural law. That is why Jesus told his apostles: If you could not heal the young boy it was because you did not have faith.

Religious faith. The state of unshakable faith

Faith can be grasped through the mind and analyzed step by step or it can be blind. Blind faith accepts everything without questioning or verifying the facts; it can short circuit reason to the point of becoming fanaticism. A reasoned faith, on the other hand, as the result of careful analysis, will never contradict reason. Every religion claims to be in exclusive possession of the truth; however, religions, which tell their followers they should have blind faith on a point of belief, are really confessing their inability to demonstrate that they are correct.

Faith cannot be imposed; that's why it is said no one can be blamed for not having faith. Faith is acquired; the only requirement is the desire to seek it out. As we search for it we should keep our eyes open: there are proofs all around us. There are so many, in fact, that, if we were to leave our pride behind long enough to acknowledge the fact that there is something greater and more powerful than us - to which we should bow before - we would find the faith we seek quite easily.

Some people find it easier to believe than others; this happens because of the progress they have made on this issue in other lives. These people have already believed and understood; and upon being reborn, they bring with them the intuition of what they know.

In other words, some people have already worked hard on acquiring and refining their faith during previous lives, while others must learn everything: they are yet to accomplish their education; but they will do so, if not in this lifetime, then in another.

Rational faith, on the other hand, by respecting and appreciating intellect and free will instead of trying to quash it (as blind faith tries to do) and by using only logic and facts with which to build its foundation, softens the skepticism of the incredulous minds. Spiritism tells us: "Unshakable faith is only the kind that can stand face to face with reason in all human epochs."

Parable of the withered fig tree

> *The next day as they were leaving Bethany, Jesus was hungry. Seeing in the distance a fig tree in leaf, he went to find out if it had any fruit. When he reached it, he found nothing but leaves, because it was not the season for figs. Then he said to the tree, "May no one ever eat fruit from you again." And his disciples heard him say it. In the morning, as they went along, they saw the fig tree withered from the roots. Peter remembered and said to Jesus, "Rabbi, look! The fig tree you cursed has withered!" "Have faith in God," Jesus answered. "I tell you the truth, if anyone says to this mountain, 'Go, throw yourself into the sea,' and does not doubt in his heart but believes that what he says will happen, it will be done for him. (Mark, chapter 11: 12-14 e 20-23)*

The dry fig tree in the parable symbolizes persons who have only the appearances of goodness, but who in reality produce nothing worthwhile. It is also the symbol of all persons who have the means to be useful but are not, and all the religions that could have brought something of value to humanity, but did not. The destiny of all the doctrines and humans who, despite their resources, produce nothing of good or value, is the same as that of the fig tree in the parable: they are reduced to nothing.

To the mediums (to whom special faculties were given) is left a very special mission: they are to use their gifts to spread the message of love and benevolence among all of humanity, never once turning away from their mission to indulge themselves in futile interests. The mediums, which are found everywhere, in all countries, among all social classes, among the rich and the poor—must use their gifts altruistically and with total abnegation in order to avoid ending up like the unfruitful fig tree. For God can take this gift away from them, if it is not put to good use and made available to everyone, or even let them become the prey of evil spirits.

In this chapter, the spirits teach:

1. That faith, hope and charity are inseparable.

2. That real faith is strong enough to stand up to the mockery of those who do not believe.

3. That sincere faith is exciting and contagious; it impresses those who do not have it and even those who do not wish to have it.

4. That the best way to show our faith and communicate it to others is through the examples of our acts and the strength of our confidence when we face the vicissitudes of life.

5. That we should not accept faith without demonstrable proof, in other words, blind faith.

6. That we should love God, believe in His promises and follow the advice of His good spirits, fully conscious of our reasons for doing so.

7. That even our search for faith should be freely chosen.

8. That the so-called miracles Jesus performed were natural effects of the power of His will and can be clearly explained by Spiritism and magnetism.

9. That there are no tendencies in human beings that are so bad that we cannot conquer them with the power of faith.

10. That magnetism is one of the greatest proofs of faith put in practice, and that it is through faith that it produces healings and other phenomena formerly known as miraculous.

11. That the capacity to perform so-called miracles comes from the development of natural human abilities.

12. That any one of us could perform such wonders if we knew our own strength and put it at the service of our will.

CHAPTER 20

WORKERS OF THE LAST HOUR

"For the kingdom of heaven is like a landowner who went out early in the morning to hire men to work in his vineyard. He agreed to pay them a denarius for the day and sent them into his vineyard." About the third hour he went out and saw others standing in the marketplace doing nothing. He told them, 'You also go and work in my vineyard, and I will pay you whatever is right.' So they went. "He went out again about the sixth hour and the ninth hour and did the same thing. About the eleventh hour he went out and found still others standing around. He asked them, 'Why have you been standing here all day long doing nothing?' "'Because no one has hired us,' they answered. "He said to them, 'You also go and work in my vineyard.' "When evening came, the owner of the vineyard said to his foreman, 'Call the workers and pay them their wages, beginning with the last ones hired and going on to the first.' "The workers who were hired about the eleventh hour came and each received a denarius. So when those came who were hired first, they expected to receive more. But each one of them also received a denarius. When they received it, they began to grumble against the landowner. 'These men who were hired last worked only one hour,' they said, 'and you have made them equal to us who have borne the burden of the work and the heat of the day.' "But he answered one of them, 'Friend, I am not being unfair to you. Didn't you agree to work for a denarius? Take your pay and go. I want to give the man who was hired last the same as I gave you. Don't I have the right to do what I want with my own money? Or are you envious because I am generous?' "So the last will be first, and the first will be last." (Matthew, chapter 20: 1-16 – see also the parable of the wedding feast", chapter 18: 1)

In this chapter the spirits teach:

1. That the worker of the last hour has a right to one's wages, since one's lateness is not due to either laziness or ill will, but to the fact he or she was waiting for someone to finally offer him or her work.

2. That most of us, Spiritists are workers of the last hour i.e., that just now we are awakening to the practice of goodness that the Gospel teaches us.

3. That the workers of the first hours were Moses and the prophets, and the workers of the following hours were the apostles, the martyrs, the founders of the Church, the wise people, and the philosophers, and finally the Spiritists that are the workers of the last hour.

4. That the workers who came later learn from the work of those who came before.

5. That many among the first workers reincarnated as Spiritists, and they can help more because of the advancement they have already achieved, returning to the work they started in previous incarnations.

6. That the Spiritists are responsible for spreading the concept of reincarnation and the elevation of spirits according to their merit, always spreading the divine word.

7. That we, Spiritists, should fight against injustice and inequity, using words of consolation, fraternity, hope and peace.

8. That we should believe in mediumistic phenomena even if we have never witnessed them.

9. That we should strive to remove from the hearts of people the impurities that withdraw them from God.

10. That it is the mission of the Spiritists to take the divine word to all, children and adults alike, whether they decide to accept it or not.

11. That many Spiritists deviate from the right path, and we must be careful so that this does not happen with us.

12. That we can recognize those who continue in the right path by the principles of true charity they teach and practice, by the large number of afflicted ones they console, for their personal impartiality, for the love they have to others, and for how sincerely they follow the law of God.

13. That those who labor for the divine work will be happy, uniting their efforts to those of their brothers.

14. That those who have pity on others, and defend and help others, that do not seek their reward in the material pleasures and the satisfaction of their own pride, will be happy.

15. That God knows how to separate those who present sincere dedication from those whose sincere dedication is only apparent.

CHAPTER 21

THERE WILL BE FALSE CHRISTS AND FALSE PROPHETS

A tree is known by its fruits

"No good tree bears bad fruit, nor does a bad tree bear good fruit. Each tree is recognized by its own fruit. People do not pick figs from thornbushes, or grapes from briers. The good man brings good things out of the good stored up in his heart, and the evil man brings evil things out of the evil stored up in his heart. For out of the overflow of his heart his mouth speaks. (Luke, chapter 6: 43-45)

"Watch out for false prophets. They come to you in sheep's clothing, but inwardly they are ferocious wolves. By their fruit you will recognize them. Do people pick grapes from thornbushes, or figs from thistles? Likewise every good tree bears good fruit, but a bad tree bears bad fruit. A good tree cannot bear bad fruit, and a bad tree cannot bear good fruit. Every tree that does not bear good fruit is cut down and thrown into the fire. Thus, by their fruit you will recognize them. (Matthew, chapter 7: 15-20)

Jesus answered: "Watch out that no one deceives you. For many will come in my name, claiming, 'I am the Christ,' and will deceive many. And many false prophets will appear and deceive many people. Because of the increase of wickedness, the love of most will grow cold, but he who stands firm to the end will be saved. At that time if anyone says to you, 'Look, here is the Christ!' or, 'There he is!' do not believe it. For false Christs and false prophets will appear and perform great signs and miracles to deceive even the elect—if that were possible. (Matthew, chapter 24: 4, 5, 11-13, 23, 24; Mark, chapter 13: 5, 6, 21, 22)

In the Gospel sense, a prophet is someone sent by God with the mission of instructing humankind and revealing the hidden things and mysteries of the spiritual life. As many people are able to foresee the future, such gift became to be attributed to prophets, although not all prophets have it.

Every phenomenon that may seem supernatural or miraculous to many is nothing but the application of the natural laws. Thus, as science advances, several occurrences at first identified as miracles may then be understood and explained.

At all times, there have always been people who explore some of their own knowledge to dominate others, to get prestige and/or to be known as sent by God. These are the false Christs and prophets Jesus referred to, and science has unmasked them along time, by revealing they were not working real miracles.

There is also another even more dangerous type of false prophets: discarnated deceitful spirits, who assume someone else's personality, pretending to be wise and therefore communicating absurd ideas. True missionaries of God can be recognized by their moral and spiritual qualities, and by the quality of their deeds, much more than by the supposed miracles they are able to perform.

Moreover, Spiritism does not work miracles or prodigies. It only reveals natural laws still unknown, which rule the relationship between material and spiritual worlds.

In this chapter, the spirits teach:

1. That the best way to distinguish false from real prophets is by examining their works and virtues.

2. That we must not entirely trust those who claim to own the truth.

3. That those sent by Jesus with the mission of spreading his doctrine follow his examples by being mild, humble and modest, and are not motivated by greed.

4. That a person's superiority or inferiority can be measured by their acts.

5. That we must open up our hearts to the lessons we learn from Spiritism and always try to progress.

6. That we must be aware of the false prophets, trying to recognize and unmask them.

7. That the real prophets, those whose mission is helping us to progress, are superior spirits, who have both intelligence and moral qualities more advanced than ours.

8. That the real prophets are recognized by their acts, whereas false prophets announce themselves as sent by God.

9. That several impostors, in the four corners of the world, claim they are sent by God.

10. That there are false prophets even among the discarnated spirits and that they deceive mediums by pretending to be someone else.

11. That these false discarnated prophets sow the seeds of discord and division, and that they may be unmasked due to such attitudes.

12. That we are able to recognize these false prophets only by using our reason when examining their communications, and that we must always repel them.

13. That when a truth must be revealed to humankind, it is usually revealed to several serious groups and mediums at the same time.

14. That the mediums and groups who consider themselves to have exclusive privilege of receiving communications of a supposed superior spirit are, actually, being importuned by some discarnated false prophet.

15. That we, Spiritists, must have prudence towards the communications we receive and that we must learn how to distinguish the good from the bad spirits, so we do not become, as well, false prophets.

CHAPTER 22
WHOM GOD HAD JOINED TOGETHER, LET NO MAN PUT APART

Some Pharisees came to him to test him. They asked, "Is it lawful for a man to divorce his wife for any and every reason?" "Haven't you read," he replied, "that at the beginning the Creator 'made them male and female,' and said, 'For this reason a man will leave his father and mother and be united to his wife, and the two will become one flesh'? So they are no longer two, but one. Therefore what God has joined together, let man not separate." "Why then," they asked, "did Moses command that a man give his wife a certificate of divorce and send her away?" Jesus replied, "Moses permitted you to divorce your wives because your hearts were hard. But it was not this way from the beginning. I tell you that anyone who divorces his wife, except for marital unfaithfulness, and marries another woman commits adultery." (Matthew, chapter 19: 3-9)

There is nothing immutable except what has come from God. Everything that is the work of humans is subject to changes. The laws of nature are the same at all times and in all countries. Human laws change according to time, place and intellectual progress. The laws governing marriage are the laws of humans, and the proof is that they are different from one country to another, and also change over time.

But the laws governing love are divine laws, and, therefore, are immutable. No human law can be above the law of God. So when Jesus says we cannot "separate what God has joined together," he refers to the law of love, and not the human law of marriage.

Such human law is, however, useful and necessary, despite it is quite variable. It exists to regulate the relationships among human beings, so that we do not live as savages. Nevertheless, nothing stops it from being in accordance with the divine law.

In this manner, loveless marriages of interest may perfectly be undone without disobeying God's laws. The divorce, when it comes about, only separates legally what was already separated. That is why it is not contrary to the divine law.

Jesus himself did not consecrate the indissolubility of marriage. Did he not say "It was because of the hardness of your hearts that Moses permitted you to divorce your wives?" He was saying that if the love between the spouses was not present along the marriage, separation might be necessary. And, when he added "but in the beginning it was not like that," he meant that in the origin of humankind, when people were not guided by greed and selfishness, and lived according to God's law, unions were based on love; that is the reason why divorces did not happen. Moreover, he said: separation could be a consequence of betrayal (adultery). But there is no adultery where sincere mutual affection exists; in this case the divorce does not contest the law of God.

Whoever does not hate his father and mother

> *Large crowds were traveling with Jesus, and turning to them he said: "If anyone comes to me and does not hate his father and mother, his wife and children, his brothers and sisters—yes, even his own life—he cannot be my disciple. And anyone who does not carry his cross and follow me cannot be my disciple. (Luke, chapter 14: 25-27; 33)*

> *"Anyone who loves his father or mother more than me is not worthy of me; anyone who loves his son or daughter more than me is not worthy of me. (Matthew, chapter 10: 37)*

The gospels were written a long time after Christ's death. Besides, when translated from one language to another, the meaning of many words might have been distorted. That is what happened with the biblical text above, and also with many other well known gospel texts. After all, Hebrew was not a rich language and contained many words with several connotations. The word "hate" from this passage from Lucas has a different meaning from that we know. Jesus would never advise any person to "hate" any one, specially their parents and family.

In order to interpret many Gospel passages, we must consider the customs and characteristics of the people from that time, in addition to the particular meaning of their languages. For this reason, a literal translation not always expresses an actual thought. To truly express such thoughts in a translation, it is often necessary to employ words that are not the exact translation of the original words.

Forsaking father, mother and children

And everyone who has left houses or brothers or sisters or father or mother or children or fields for my sake will receive a hundred times as much and will inherit eternal life. (Matthew, chapter 19: 29)

Peter said to him, "We have left all we had to follow you!" "I tell you the truth," Jesus said to them, "no one who has left home or wife or brothers or parents or children for the sake of the kingdom of God will fail to receive many times as much in this age and, in the age to come, eternal life." (Luke, chapter 18: 28-30)

Still another said, "I will follow you, Lord; but first let me go back and say good-by to my family." Jesus replied, "No one who puts his hand to the plow and looks back is fit for service in the kingdom of God." (Luke, chapter 9: 61-62)

The words from this passage cannot be read literally as well, as they would not be in accordance with the substance of Jesus' doctrine, which teaches to value love among people and families. We should understand these words by their thoughts, which was obviously this: "the interests of future life should be placed above all human interests and considerations."

Thus, Christ wanted to show us there are obligations more important than others and, above all, we must prepare ourselves to the future life. The separation from our beloved ones itself is, many times, necessary to our moral progress (ours and theirs). After all, the true bonds of affection are spiritual, not physical. Therefore, these bonds cannot be broken by physical separation and not even by the death of the body.

Let the dead bury their own dead

He said to another man, "Follow me." But the man replied, "Lord, first let me go and bury my father." Jesus said to him,

"Let the dead bury their own dead, but you go and proclaim the kingdom of God." (Luke, chapter 9: 59-60)

Of course that when Jesus said, "let the dead bury their own dead" (and for the same reasons we have mentioned above), his intention was not to condemn the desire of a son to bury his father. This passage has a very profound meaning that can only be understood with a more complete knowledge of the spirit life. In fact, life in the spirit world is the true life; it is the normal life of the spirit.

We, Spiritists, are aware that the body is only a "garment" of the spirit, rough and transitory, a true "prison" from which it is happy to be free. This way, Jesus meant that the respect for the dead must not be addressed to the matter (or to the dead body), but to the spirit. He recommended, in fact, that we must not worry about the body, but about the spirit, teaching people around us that the true life is the spirit life.

I have not come to bring peace but division

"Do not suppose that I have come to bring peace to the earth. I did not come to bring peace, but a sword. For I have come to turn" 'a man against his father, a daughter against her mother, a daughter-in-law against her mother-in-law - a man's enemies will be the members of his own household.' (Matthew, chapter 10: 34-36)

"I have come to bring fire on the earth, and how I wish it were already kindled! But I have a baptism to undergo, and how distressed I am until it is completed! Do you think I came to bring peace on earth? No, I tell you, but division. From now on there will be five in one family divided against each other, three against two and two against three. They will be divided, father against son and son against father, mother against daughter and daughter against mother, mother-in-law against daughter-in-law and daughter-in-law against mother-in-law." (Luke, chapter 12: 49-53)

Could it be that Jesus, the personification of kindness and goodness, who always preached love to our fellow creatures, had said such words? Yes, He said that, and, in fact, His words show great wisdom.

Jesus came to earth to preach a new idea – which, as every new idea, would be opposed and hated, would contest old beliefs and discontent and disturb many people. His doctrine would change everything and that is why he was sacrificed. His opponents thought that by killing Jesus they would also kill his ideas; however, this never happened, as his ideas strongly survived until nowadays because they represent the truth.

Nonetheless, many fought his doctrine, many were the battles his apostles had to engage in, and many were the victims from those fights in favor of Jesus' truths. Great material interests began to be contested and innumerous people defended the false judgment, but the time had come to spread those new ideas and that is why they triumph and prosper until the present days.

Unfortunately, through time, the followers of the new doctrine have interpreted Jesus' words in different ways, originating countless sects, all of them claiming that they alone possess the truth. Many of them forgot the essence of Jesus' doctrine – charity, fraternity and love to our fellow creatures – and started to dispute, trying to suffocate those who had different ideas. That was when fires, tortures and religious wars began to rise... and all this in the name of God!

But is this Christianity's fault? Of course not! Jesus never sowed the seed of discord; his words were always about love and union. He always preached that we are all brothers and sisters, and that we should always love each other and our enemies as well, as it is our duty to do good unto others, even to those who oppress us. Therefore, it is not Christianity's fault, but wrong interpretations' (always results of personal interests). However, such things were unavoidable because they were connected to the inferiority of human nature.

Thus, when Christ said he had not come to bring peace, but division, he was saying that his doctrine would not be established peacefully. He was referring to events such as bloody battles among people of different beliefs, many times from the same family, which happened in the name of this doctrine. When he said he had come "to bring fire on the earth", he was saying his message would come to purify the planet, the same way fire free the fields from weed.

Later, Jesus would send us the Consoler, the Spirit of Truth, which is Spiritism. Therefore, Spiritism came to explain the true meaning of Jesus' words and to accomplish his promises, to establish true fraternity among all.

Like Jesus, on its path Spiritism encounters pride, selfishness, greed, ambition, and blind fanaticism, which result in great difficulties and oppression. However, the current spiritists have to endure are of a moral nature, and their end is near.

CHAPTER 24

DO NOT HIDE YOUR LAMP UNDER A BUSHEL

A lamp under a bushel – Why Jesus speaks in parables

Neither do people light a lamp and put it under a bowl. Instead they put it on its stand, and it gives light to everyone in the house. (Matthew, chapter 5: 15)

"No one lights a lamp and hides it in a jar or puts it under a bed. Instead, he puts it on a stand, so that those who come in can see the light. For there is nothing hidden that will not be disclosed, and nothing concealed that will not be known or brought out into the open. (Luke, chapter 8: 16-17)

The disciples came to him and asked, "Why do you speak to the people in parables?" He replied, "The knowledge of the secrets of the kingdom of heaven has been given to you, but not to them. Whoever has will be given more, and he will have an abundance. Whoever does not have, even what he has will be taken from him. This is why I speak to them in parables: "Though seeing, they do not see; though hearing, they do not hear or understand. In them is fulfilled the prophecy of Isaiah: "'You will be ever hearing but never understanding; you will be ever seeing but never perceiving. For this people's heart has become calloused; they hardly hear with their ears, and they have closed their eyes. Otherwise they might see with their eyes, hear with their ears, understand with their hearts and turn, and I would heal them.' (Matthew, chapter 13: 10-15)

To put a lamp under a table means hiding the light; we may be surprise to hear Jesus say that one should not put "a lamp under a table", when many times he himself used to hide the meaning of his words through symbolism in parables.

If one should not put "a lamp under a table", why then Jesus spoke through parables? The last passage from Mathew answers such question. In that passage, Jesus explains he must speak that way so that people from his time, still not much instructed or mature, would understand his words. Everything happens in the right moment. This means that, sooner or later, all the truths will be understood and people themselves (as they evolve and develop) will search for these truths.

Many religions have always insisted on keeping mysteries and forbidding their followers to study or question these mysteries, aiming at dominating them. This is "hiding the light under a bowl", that is, hiding the truth. But the science and humans' intelligence have been improving to follow Jesus's words, when he said "there is nothing hidden that will not be disclosed". There is still a lot to be disclosed on earth, therefore, the more advanced is a world, the more mysteries will be disclosed.

When Jesus spoke to less instructed people, he made use of parables, although important aspects such as charity and humbleness as basic conditions for salvation were always approached in a very clear way, so that simpler people were not confused. In turn, when he spoke to his disciples (more instructed than ordinary people), he could speak with more complexity and that is why he said, "to those who already have much more will be given,"

Many things were not revealed, however, in a precise manner not even to the disciples. Only science and Spiritism would reveal them later. But, of course, not everything has been revealed to us and there is a logical explanation for this: there is a right moment for everything, each idea needs to be developed, to be spread and to be accepted before a new idea comes out.

Do not go to the gentiles

These twelve Jesus sent out with the following instructions: "Do not go among the Gentiles or enter any town of the Samaritans. Go rather to the lost sheep of Israel. As you go,

preach this message: 'The kingdom of heaven is near.'
(Matthew, chapter 10: 5-7)

In this passage from Matthew, Jesus tells his disciples that before worrying about the gentiles (that is, those who were not aware of the divine truths), they should first "go rather to the lost sheep of Israel" (that is, the Jews, who believed in only one God and had been waiting for the Messiah), which was a lighter task for the beginning of the works. The same can be advised to Spiritists, who should first disseminate the doctrine among people of good-will, for those prepared to receive the divine message, dealing with skeptics and resistant people later (who will also believe at the right time).

The healthy do not need a doctor

While Jesus was having dinner at Matthew's house, many tax collectors and "sinners" came and ate with him and his disciples. When the Pharisees saw this, they asked his disciples, "Why does your teacher eat with tax collectors and 'sinners'?" On hearing this, Jesus said, "It is not the healthy who need a doctor, but the sick. But go and learn what this means: 'I desire mercy, not sacrifice.' For I have not come to call the righteous, but sinners." (Matthew, chapter 9: 10-12)

Jesus always attempted to be close to those who needed him: the poor, the sufferer, and the ignorant of the divine truth. And this applies to Spiritism as for mediumship. Many find it strange that mediumship are, many times, granted to unworthy people, capable of making a bad use of it, but this is not uncommon at all. Mediumship is connected to an organic disposition (just as that of seeing, listening and speaking) and anyone can have it. We are free to choose how to use all our capacities (including mediumship) but we will be held responsible if we abuse of them.

Mediumship is granted to rich and poor, good and bad, and is always useful for those who have it. It can, for instance, help a bad person, since it provides one with good advices and orientation from superior spirits. And, if this person uses it wrongly, they mat lose it or end up as its victim, being besieged by obscure spirits. After all, mediumship is an ability to communicate with spirits, whether they are good or bad. It all depends on the will and moral qualities of each medium.

The courage of faith

"Whoever acknowledges me before men, I will also acknowledge him before my Father in heaven. But whoever disowns me before men, I will disown him before my Father in heaven. (Matthew, chapter 10: 32-33)

If anyone is ashamed of me and my words, the Son of Man will be ashamed of him when he comes in his glory and in the glory of the Father and of the holy angels. (Luke, chapter 9: 26)

Denying our own opinion, for fear of consequences, is always a sign of weakness. But there are cases this is more than just weakness: it is cowardice; it is like running away from a good and fair fight. Jesus then reminds us that, if we are afraid or ashamed to admit our beliefs and convictions in his doctrine, we shall not be worthy of Heaven. The same applies to Spiritists, who sow on earth what they will seed in spiritual life, whether this is the result of their courage or their cowardice.

Carry your cross – He who will save his life shall lose it

Blessed are you when men hate you, when they exclude you and insult you and reject your name as evil, because of the Son of Man. "Rejoice in that day and leap for joy, because great is your reward in heaven. For that is how their fathers treated the prophets. (Lucas, chapter 6: 22-23)

Then he called the crowd to him along with his disciples and said: "If anyone would come after me, he must deny himself and take up his cross and follow me. For whoever wants to save his life will lose it, but whoever loses his life for me and for the gospel will save it. What good is it for a man to gain the whole world, yet forfeit his soul? (Mark, chapter 8: 34-36; Luke, chapter 9: 23-25; Matthew, chapter 10: 38-39; John, chapter 12: 25-26)

Differently from what we may think, being victim of hatred and injustice may cause us happiness. Because, as Jesus said, when we are somehow mistreated or wronged by someone, it is a great opportunity to prove the sincerity of our principles and faith. That is, we can gain points in Heaven. Thus, it is natural that we feel sorry for their iniquity, but we should never curse them for the harm they caused us.

When Christ says we must take up his cross and follow him, he advises us to bear courageously the suffering we may go through for following his doctrine, being certain that we will have future rewarding.

CHAPTER 25

SEEK AND YOU WILL FIND

Help yourself and heaven will help you

"Ask and it will be given to you; seek and you will find; knock and the door will be opened to you. For everyone who asks receives; he who seeks finds; and to him who knocks, the door will be opened.

"Which of you, if his son asks for bread, will give him a stone? Or if he asks for a fish, will give him a snake? If you, then, though you are evil, know how to give good gifts to your children, how much more will your Father in heaven give good gifts to those who ask him! (Matthew, chapter 7: 7-11)

To say "seek and you will find" is the same as saying "help yourself then heaven will come to your aid." It is the principle of the law of labor and the law of progress, since progress results from labor. In the beginning of times, the human beings just used their intelligence to get the means to survive. But God has given them the incessant desire to better themselves, it is this desire that drives them to seek out means of improving their situation, and from this desire we see progresses, such as in science, which provide a greater advancement of their intelligence and moral qualities.

Despite the evident collective progresses, it is difficult to notice individual improvements in a lifetime. How then, could humankind progress without the preexistence and re-existence of the soul? If souls were always young, if evolution had to start from scratch every time, collective progress would not exist. The explanation is reincarnation: souls reincarnate in new bodies, always better and more advanced than before. That is how material and spiritual evolution of human collectivity happens.

And work is necessary for such evolution, since we are inheritors of our own actions, that is, we will have the merit and be rewarded for what we may have done. For this reason, the spirits do not spare us to make all the efforts we can, by not giving us everything done. These efforts are the requirement for our progress. We face obstacles that we must overcome on our own. Spirits give us strength, but it is up to us to use it or not. That was what Jesus meant by saying "ask and it will be given to you; seek and you will find; knock and the door will be opened to you." That is, whenever we ask with faith and hope, we will get the strength, assistance and good advices from the spirits, but we must cooperate with our own efforts and work.

Look at the birds of the air

"Do not store up for yourselves treasures on earth, where moth and rust destroy, and where thieves break in and steal. But store up for yourselves treasures in heaven, where moth and rust do not destroy, and where thieves do not break in and steal. For where your treasure is, there your heart will be also.

"Therefore I tell you, do not worry about your life, what you will eat or drink; or about your body, what you will wear. Is not life more important than food, and the body more important than clothes? Look at the birds of the air; they do not sow or reap or store away in barns, and yet your heavenly Father feeds them. Are you not much more valuable than they? Who of you by worrying can add a single hour to his life? "And why do you worry about clothes? See how the lilies of the field grow. They do not labor or spin. Yet I tell you that not even Solomon in all his splendor was dressed like one of these. If that is how God clothes the grass of the field, which is here today and tomorrow is thrown into the fire, will he not much more clothe you, O you of little faith? So do not worry, saying, 'What shall we eat?' or 'What shall we drink?' or 'What shall we wear?' For the pagans run after all these things, and your heavenly Father knows that you need them. But seek first his kingdom and his righteousness, and all these things will be given to you as well. Therefore do not worry

about tomorrow, for tomorrow will worry about itself. Each day has enough trouble of its own. (Matthew, chapter 6: 19-21; 25-34)

Contrariwise of what it may seem at the first glance when we read this passage, Jesus did not advise us to be stagnant, passively waiting things to fall from heaven. By such words, He meant we can trust divine Providence, who never abandons those who trust, but in turn we must do our part through our work and efforts. God knows our necessities and tries to take care of them, but many times we wish more than it is necessary and, in this case, we cannot be attended.

Earth is capable of producing enough to feed all its inhabitants; scarcity and hunger are results of our incapability to administrate wealth in a benevolent and just way, based on the love to our fellow creatures. When fraternity prevails among us, everyone will have the necessary and there will be enough for each of us. Moreover, according to Jesus' advices, we should always give more importance to spiritual than to material wealth.

However, there is no human law capable of proclaiming fraternity and charity; selfishness will always win while these virtues do not inhabit in our hearts – and it is Spiritism's mission to place them there.

Provide not gold in your purse

Do not take along any gold or silver or copper in your belts; take no bag for the journey, or extra tunic, or sandals or a staff; for the worker is worth his keep. "Whatever town or village you enter, search for some worthy person there and stay at his house until you leave. As you enter the home, give it your greeting. If the home is deserving, let your peace rest on it; if it is not, let your peace return to you. If anyone will not welcome you or listen to your words, shake the dust off your feet when you leave that home or town. I tell you the truth, it will be more bearable for Sodom and

Gomorrah on the day of judgment than for that town.
(Matthew, chapter 10: 9-15)

By saying this, Jesus was teaching his disciples to trust in Providence. By having nothing, they could not tempt the greed of those who received them. It was a way to distinguish the benevolent people from the selfish and self-seeking ones, once the guest would have no means to afford the accommodation.

Thus, benevolent ones (or those who offer shelter even when not getting paid for that) would be worthy of hearing their peace wishes. But Jesus did not advise the disciples to react against those who did not want to receive them; he just advised them to go somewhere else and look for people of goodwill.

That is what Spiritism tells its followers today: to not force anyone to convert to Spiritism, to respect those who think differently, to kindly welcome those who approach, and to not react against those who reject them.

CHAPTER 26

GIVE FREELY WHAT YOU HAVE RECEIVED FREELY

The gift of healing

Heal the sick, raise the dead, cleanse those who have leprosy, drive out demons. Freely you have received, freely give. (Matthew, chapter 10: 8)

We cannot charge for things we have not paid for. Therefore, the gift of healing and other mediumistic abilities, freely received, cannot be transformed into paid objects or trade, or a way of one earning a living.

Paid prayers

While all the people were listening, Jesus said to his disciples, "Beware of the teachers of the law. They like to walk around in flowing robes and love to be greeted in the marketplaces and have the most important seats in the synagogues and the places of honor at banquets. They devour widows' houses and for a show make lengthy prayers. Such men will be punished most severely." (Luke, chapter 20: 45-47; Mark, chapter 12: 38-40; Matthew, chapter 23: 14)

Prayer is an act of charity that must come from the heart, and no one should charge for it. God does not sell the benefits it gives us and does not allow anyone to establish a price for His justice, which exists for all, rich and poor alike. Paid prayers have no value. We should not pay another person to pray for us, because it is our fervor that makes them effective.

The merchants expelled from the temple

On reaching Jerusalem, Jesus entered the temple area and began driving out those who were buying and selling there. He overturned the tables of the money changers and the benches of those selling doves, and would not allow anyone to carry merchandise through the temple courts. And as he taught them, he said, "Is it not written: 'My house will be called a house of prayer for all nations'? But you have made it 'a den of robbers.' The chief priests and the teachers of the law heard this and began looking for a way to kill him, for they feared him, because the whole crowd was amazed at his teaching. (Mark, chapter 11: 15-18; Matthew, chapter 21: 12-13)

When Jesus expelled the merchants from the temple, he was condemning the selling of holy things, like the blessing and forgiveness of God or an easy entrance to the kingdom of heaven.

Mediums have received a free gift from God: that of being the interpreters of spirits for the instruction of humankind, to show them the pathway to the good and to lead them to faith. They cannot sell messages, since they are not the result of their own effort and work (they are only intermediaries of something that comes from the spirit world). Furthermore, God wants the divine truths to reach rich and poor, regardless of their ability to pay. And that is the reason why mediumship is not a privilege, and exists everywhere.

The good spirits would never accept to communicate through mediums that sell their own mediumship, and that charge for their "services". After all, the first condition to receive their assistance is humility, selflessness and total lack of interest for personal gains. Only inferior minds lend themselves to such kind of communications that are never serious or sincere.

Therefore, mediumship cannot be turned into a profession, as it is very different from the talents achieved

158

through study and work. It does not exist without the cooperation of spirits, and can be taken away at any time. It does not belong to the medium, and therefore one cannot do with it as one pleases. Spiritism teaches us that mediumship is a mission.

Mediumship is something sacred and it should be practiced in a good and respectful way. There is one type of mediumship that requires this condition even more: the healing mediumship. Healing mediums retransmit healing fluids from the good spirits, and a price cannot be put upon these. Jesus and his Apostles, although poor, did not charge for the cure they obtained.

So then, the mediums that do not have the financial means to support themselves should go and seek resources somewhere else other than in mediumship, and if necessary, devote to it only the spare time they have available.

CHAPTER 27

ASK AND IT SHALL BE GIVEN

The characteristics of prayer

"And when you pray, do not be like the hypocrites, for they love to pray standing in the synagogues and on the street corners to be seen by men. I tell you the truth, they have received their reward in full. But when you pray, go into your room, close the door and pray to your Father, who is unseen. Then your Father, who sees what is done in secret, will reward you. And when you pray, do not keep on babbling like pagans, for they think they will be heard because of their many words. Do not be like them, for your Father knows what you need before you ask him. (Matthew, chapter 6: 5-8)

And when you stand praying, if you hold anything against anyone, forgive him, so that your Father in heaven may forgive you your sins." (Mark, chapter 11: 25-26)

To some who were confident of their own righteousness and looked down on everybody else, Jesus told this parable: "Two men went up to the temple to pray, one a Pharisee and the other a tax collector. The Pharisee stood up and prayed about himself: 'God, I thank you that I am not like other men—robbers, evildoers, adulterers—or even like this tax collector. I fast twice a week and give a tenth of all I get.' "But the tax collector stood at a distance. He would not even look up to heaven, but beat his breast and said, 'God, have mercy on me, a sinner.' "I tell you that this man, rather than the other, went home justified before God. For everyone who exalts himself will be humbled, and he who humbles himself will be exalted." (Luke, chapter 18: 9-14)

All these parts of the gospel teach one fundamental thing: how to pray. As instructed by Jesus, when we pray we should not make it obvious to others; to pray in secret is the best in the eyes of God. The prayer doesn't need to be long and complicated, because it is not by the amount of the words that our prayers have that they will be granted, but by their sincerity and fervor. Before praying, we should forgive our enemies, so that God can also forgive us. Finally, when praying we should look at our conscience in order to recognize our mistakes and defects, always assuming a humble attitude.

The effectiveness of prayer

Therefore I tell you, whatever you ask for in prayer, believe that you have received it, and it will be yours. (Mark, chapter 11: 24)

There are those who think that prayer does not help because God knows our needs and because the universe would be governed by immutable laws that could not be changed by our simple request. Surely these laws exist, but there is much in life that can be corrected depending on our attitudes. If it were like that, than the individuals would be passive beings, without initiative and free will, which is not true. Therefore, it is quite possible that God may grant some of our requests without hurting any immutable law.

But when Jesus says that whatever we ask in prayer, believing that we will achieve it, we will really end up getting it, he is not saying that God will grant us anything we ask for, without seeing if this will be for our own good. As we see only the present moment, oftentimes we do not understand that God cannot rid us from some pain, because this suffering will be useful for our future happiness. It's like the surgeon who allows the patient to suffer an operation that will cure him or her.

What God will always give us is courage and strength to face the difficult situations, along with patience and resignation. He will also send good ideas and inspiration through the good spirits, expecting us to do our part. The maxim, "Help yourself and Heaven will help you" summarizes it well. What does not help is to wish to be saved by a miracle, without using any effort of our own, because, in order for salvation to be of value, the merit has to be ours.

The action of prayer – Transmission of thought

Prayer is an invocation through which our mind communicates with the superior spirits. We can pray to ask for something, to give thanks or to praise; we can pray for ourselves, for others, for the living and for the dead.

Spiritism makes the act of prayer clear by explaining that it is transmitted through thought. All incarnates and discarnates are immersed in the universal fluid, which occupies space. Thought is transmitted through this fluid. So, when our thought is directed to someone (or when someone directs their thoughts to us), either on earth or in space, from an incarnate to a discarnate being, or vice-versa, a fluidic current is established between them, which transmit the thought to one another. The stronger the thought and the greater the will, the greater the energy of this current will be. This is how spirits communicate among themselves, how they transmit their inspirations to us, and how contacts are established at a distance between incarnates. And that's what happens with prayers; but they are always subordinated to the will of God.

Prayer brings us the assistance of the good spirits, who help us in our good decisions and inspire positive ideas. Through prayer we acquire moral strength to overcome difficulties and come back to the right path, or to keep ourselves on the right track.

The ills of life fall into two categories: first are the ills we cannot avoid, and second those that we bring for ourselves due to our mistakes or our excesses. But the number in the second group is bigger than those of the first, and is a result of our disobedience to God's law. Many diseases that we experience are the result of abuses committed. If we placed a limit on our ambition, we would not fear ruin. If we did not want to ascend higher than we are capable of, we would not fear a downfall. If we did not cause harm to anyone, we would not fear revenge.

The effect of a prayer is drawing inspiration from the spirits, and then get strength to resist the bad thoughts that, if put to work, can bring us harmful consequences. The spirits though, as they listen to our prayers, are not preventing the fulfillment of God's laws, but they are helping us to avoid the bad thoughts that can cause us harm, driving our free will. That is, through prayer we ask them good advices, but we keep our freedom to follow them or not, and that's exactly the way God wants it to be. That way we can be held accountable for our own actions and we will have merit in choosing between the good and the evil.

The prayer of a good person is always more valuable and effective than the prayer of a bad person, who cannot pray with the same fervor and the same confidence. But by no means someone who thinks he or she is not good enough should stop praying for the good of others, because God always takes into account the good intentions of the one who prays. Their fervor and trust in God are a first step in the return to goodness.

The power of prayer is in the thoughts, not in the words. It doesn't depend on the place or time. One can pray anywhere and at any time, alone or in a group. Prayer in a group is more powerful when all those who pray are joined by the same heartfelt thought and have the same purpose.

Intelligible prayers

If then I do not grasp the meaning of what someone is saying, I am a foreigner to the speaker, and he is a foreigner to me. For if I pray in a tongue, my spirit prays, but my mind is unfruitful. If you are praising God with your spirit, how can one who finds himself among those who do not understand say "Amen" to your thanksgiving, since he does not know what you are saying? You may be giving thanks well enough, but the other man is not edified. (Paul, 1 Corinthians, chapter 14: 11, 14, 16 and 17)

A prayer is only as good as the thoughts connected with it, and it is impossible to connect a thought to words that are not understood. Prayers spoken in an incomprehensible language are only a group of words that say nothing to the spirit.

If words are not understood, they cannot reveal ideas. Thus, there is very little use in repeating a prayer mechanically, without understanding what it means, since to God what is important is the sincerity that He notices in our thoughts when we pray.

Prayers for the dead and for suffering spirits

The prayers for the suffering spirits bring them relief and can really reduce their suffering. When we pray for these spirits, they feel less unhappy and abandoned, because they see that there are people who care about them. In addition, our prayers may cheer them up, bringing in them the desire to improve themselves through repentance and reparation, and our prayers can even take their minds away from thoughts of evil.

Some people do not believe in prayers for the dead, because they think there are only two alternatives for the soul: to be saved or be condemned to eternal punishment, and in either case prayer is useless. But even if the soul could have only one of these two alternatives wouldn't be charitable to pray for the soul? If one of our main obligations is to love one another wouldn't praying for others be a way to practice this love?

Some people think that prayers do not help, as God would not change His decisions based on requests from people. That way, we could ask nothing to Him, and we would have only to accept His decisions and to worship Him. Those who have that understanding about the immutability of the divine law believe that remorse and repentance change nothing, and that the desire to improve by a person is useless. Thus, that person would be doomed to live forever in the wrongdoing.

But the law of God is more just and merciful, and can be summarized as follows:

- People always bear the consequences of their wrongs.

- The severity of the punishment is proportional to the gravity of the wrong.

- The duration of the atonement depends on the repentance of the guilty and on one's return to the good.

- Once the guilty beg for mercy, God hears them and sends them hope.

- Simple regret for the evil committed is not enough.

- There must be reparation for the harm caused, through trials that make it possible the practice of good.

- It is in people's hands their own destiny - their suffering and happiness depend on their willingness to do good.

Such is the law, an immutable law in conformance to the goodness and justice of God, since it allows spirits who are unhappy to save themselves, under these conditions.

Salvation then is always possible, provided there is willingness, strength and courage, things that our prayers can inspire to the suffering spirits.

Then, instead of asking God to depart from the divine law, we become the instruments for carrying out God's law of love and charity.

In this chapter, spirits teach:

1. That prayer is recommended for every human being, and should be done every day as we wake up.

2. That prayer has no formula, that praying is not about mechanically repeating phrases, but directing our thoughts to God with humility and gratitude.

3. That when praying we may ask for what we need, however that being what we truly need.

4. That we should ask for patience, resignation, strength and faith when facing our every day tests, but that there is no use in asking for joy and wealth, or wanting that our lives' tests finish before the due time.

5. That if before asking for something else, we ask for our moral improvement, consolations will be sent by God.

6. That we should always pray, and that praying every day is a duty not to be forgotten.

7. That helping others with any physical or moral need is an act of loving God.

8. That showing gratitude to God could mean either thanking Him for something good that happened to us or for something bad that we have managed to avoid.

9. That our prayers should demonstrate repentance, either by asking for forgiveness for our wrongdoings, by asking for strength so that we can avoid repeat the wrongdoing, or yet by asking for courage so we can repair the consequences of our errors.

10. That the time or the place of our prayers is not important, what counts is what comes from the bottom of our hearts.

11. That having faith makes us feel good and leads our soul to repentance and prayer.

12. That praying brings us close to the good spirits and takes us to the path that leads to God

Laura Bergallo writes for the young audience. She has already published nine books and has three more to be released in 2009. She also has a Bachelor's degree in Social Communication and edits scientific publications.

Her book *The Creature* ("A Criatura") won the Adolfo Aizen Prize/2006 by the Brazilian Union of Writers, as the best youth book of 2004/2005.

Her book *Alice in the mirror* ("Alice no espelho") won the Jabuti Prize-2007 in youth category and was selected to be part of the FNLIJ Catalogue of the 44th Bologna Children's Book Fair.

Her book *Operation Wormhole* ("Operação Buraco de Minhoca") – published by DCL, 2008 - has been selected by the Program for More Culture (Programa Mais Cultura) by the Federal Government and National Library of Brazil, to be distributed in libraries and reading points all over the country.

Published books for young readers:

The four corners of the world (Os quatro cantos do mundo) - (for children) – published by Shogun-Arte, 1986 - This book was selected to the 'Youth-Children's Literature Week', promoted by Petrobras and Macaé City Hall (RJ) in 1987.

A Ghost Story – (Uma História de Fantasma) - (spiritist book) - published by LerBem (Spiritism for Children and Youth Collection), 2001 (sold out) – re-edited in 2008 and published by Lachâtre. **Translated to English by the Spiritist Alliance for Books in 2010 – www.sgny.org**

The Spirit's Book for Young Adults and Beginners – (O Livrinho dos Espíritos) - (spiritist book), published by LerBem (Spiritism for Children and Youth Collection), 2002 and 2004 (sold out) –

re-edited in 2007 and published by Léon Denis. **Published in English by the Spiritist Alliance for Books, in 2010.**

Also released in France, 2008, by Cesak-Paris, under the title of *Le Petit Livre des Esprits.*

The Gospel according to Spiritism for Young Adults and Beginners (O Evangelho Segundo o Espiritismo para o Jovem Leitor) – (spiritist book) – Lachâtre Publisher. **Published in English by the Spiritist Alliance for Books, in 2010.**

A Train to Another (?) World (Um Trem para Outro (?) Mundo) – published by Saraiva (Jabuti Collection), 2002

This book has been selected to the 'Motion Reading Program' ("Programa Leitura em Movimento"), by Petrópolis City Hall (RJ)

There's an elephant in my bedroom (Tem um elefante no meu quarto) - (for children) – published by Franco (Reading for Pleasure Collection), 2003

The Creature (A Criatura) – published by SM (Steamboat Collection), 2005 - This book won the Adolfo Aizen Prize/2006, by the Brazilian Union of Writers, as the best youth book of 2004 and 2005.

Alice in the Mirror (Alice no Espelho) – published by SM (Muriqui Collection), 2006 - This book has won the renowned Jabuti Prize, in the youth category and has been selected to the FNLIJ of the Bologna's Children Book Fair

The Disappearance Camera (A Câmera do Sumiço) - published by DCL, 2007

Books for Adolescents in production:

The witch and the supernerd (A bruxa e o supernerd) – DCL Publisher

Carioquinha – (for children) – Rocco Publisher

Television scripts:

In Pursuit of the Shadow (Em busca da Sombra) – published in the book '13 Magical Scripts', organized by Luiz Carlos Maciel – Booklink Publisher, 2002

LAURA BERGALLO IS A MEMBER OF THE ASSOCIATION OF WRITERS AND ILLUSTRATORS OF YOUTH-CHILDREN LITERATURE (AEILIJ)

Made in the USA
Lexington, KY
21 October 2011